Abortion, Birth Control And Surrogate Parenting

An Islamic Perspective

By

Abul Fadl Mohsin Ebrahim

ISBN-0-89259-081-5

Dr. A.F. Mohsin Ebrahim, currently resident in South Africa, hails from the Seychelles. After completion of his secondary education, he pursued studies at the Aleemiyah Institute, Karachi, Pakistan – founded by Maulana Dr. Muhammad Fazl-ur-Rahman Ansari (R.A.). He obtained a B.Th. from Al-Azhar University, Cairo, Egypt. Back in Seychelles in 1977, he formed the Muslim youth branch of the Islamic Society of Seychelles, founded the 'Iqra' Monthly Magazine, and campaigned for the construction of Seychelles' first Masjid. In 1982, he enrolled for the Masters program in Religion at Temple University, Philadelphia, U.S.A., and obtained an M.A. degree in Religion. He worked for his doctoral degree under the supervision of Professor Isma'il al Faruqi and was awarded one in religion with specialization in Islamic Studies in May, 1986. He is at present working as a lecturer in Islamic Studies at the University of Durban-Westville, South Africa.

To my beloved parents
for
their unceasing support, love, and affection

CONTENTS

ACKNOWLEDGMENTS

I am indebted to many people in the completion of this work. First, I would like to record my deep gratitude to my Ustadh al Shahid Dr. Isma'il R. al Faruqi (RA) for his guidance, undivided attention, and continuous encouragement. I am also grateful to al Shahidah Dr. Lois Lamya' al Faruqi (R.A), who taught us Islamic Art, for her interest and care for our welfare during our stay in Philadelphia.

My heart-felt gratitude is also due to Dr. Seyyed Hossein Nasr and Dr. John C. Raines for their assistance, genuine criticism, and valuable suggestions. I would like to thank Dr. David Smith in the Department of General Internal Medicine, Temple University Hospital, for reading the dissertation and providing some valuable suggestions.

For preparatory work, I am indebted to the Scholarship Committee of the Department of Religion, Temple University, and the Graduate School for the tuition remission allotted to me for the Fall 1983 and Spring 1984 semesters, and to the International Institute of Islamic Thought, Washington D.C., for the financial assistance granted to me between August 1983 and May 1984.

My gratitude also goes to Dr. G. Sloyan, Chairman of the Department of Religion, to Dr. G. Spiegler, Dr. R. Wright, Dr. N. Samuelson, Dr. T. Dean, Dr. B. Yadav, and to all faculty members and staff of the Department of Religion for the cooperation and assistance rendered to me during my study at Temple University. I would like to express my thanks to Dr. Syed Salman Nadvi, Professor and Head of the Department of Islamic Studies, University of Durban-Westville, Maulana Ahmad Khalil Aziz, Lecturer in the Department of Arabic, Urdu and Persian, University Durban-Westville, South Africa, Professor Ali Musa, Head of the Department of Pediatrics, University of Natal, South Africa, Dr. Goolam Hoosein, a specialist in urology, and Dr. M. Haneef Khatree, a gynecologist, for their valuable suggestions.

My thanks are also due to the small Muslim community in the Seychelles for their moral support, and to Sufi Muhammad Zaman Marwat, Hafiz Ghaffar Khan, and Syed Ghulam Nabi Fai, as well as all other Muslim students of Temple University and Department of Religion for their friendship and hospitality.

I extend my sincere gratitude to my family. I thank my beloved parents for their unceasing support, love, and affection, my grandfather, uncles, aunts, brothers, sisters, and my wife's family for their encouragement, and my wife and children for their patience and understanding during the period of my study and research.

My brother, Salim, assisted me in making necessary alterations on the computer. I am thankful to him, and to Dr. Anwar Hoosen for their help. Finally, I am grateful to the American Trust Publications for publishing this book. Above all, I am eternally indebted to the Almighty Allah, SWT, for the accomplishment of this work. Wa ma tawfiqi illa billah.

TRANSLITERATION

Arabic Letter	Transliteration	Diacritical Signs Short Vowels		
أ	ʼ	Fathah	َ	a
ب	b	Dammah	ُ	u
ت	t	Kasrah	ِ	i
ث	th			
ج	j			
ح	h	**Long Vowels**		
خ	kh	Alif Mamdudah or	آ	
د	d	or Ya Mamdudah	يٰ	ā
ذ	dh	Waw Sakin preceded		
ر	r	by Dammah		ū
ز	z	Ya Sakin preceded		
س	s	by Kasrah		ī
ش	sh			
ص	s	**Dipthongs**		
ض	ḍ	Waw Masdudah		
		preceded by Damah	ُوّ	uww
ط	ṭ	Waw Masdudah		
ظ	ẓ	preceded by Fathah		aww
ع	ʻ	Waw Sakin preceded	َوّ	
غ	gh	by Fathah		aw
ف	f	Ya Mushaddad	َوْ	
ق	q	preceded by Fathah		ayy
ك	k	Ya Mushaddad	َيّ	
ل	l	preceded by Kasrah		iyy
م	m	Ya Sakin preceded	ِيّ	
ن	n	by Fathah		ay
و	w		َيْ	
هـ	h			
ي	y			
ة	ah			
ال	(article) al even before the antepalatals.			

INTRODUCTION

Biotechnological innovations relating to birth control, infertility, and abortion increasingly are posing moral challenges. These issues are directly related to human life. All human life is regulated by the teachings of the Qur'an and the *Sunnah* of the Prophet Muhammad (SAWS). Our actions are considered proper or right if they conform to their broad teachings and improper or wrong if they contradict either the letter or the spirit of their teachings. This book focuses on the teachings of the Qur'an and the relevant *ahadith* pertaining to the beginning of human life, the sanctity of married life, and sanctions for the termination of human life. The objective is to analyze the relevant injunctions and present them in a systematic way in order better to assess the legality of such biotechnical measures under the *Shari'ah*.

First we shall introduce the basis of Islamic ethics as background for discussing some more specific concepts of health care, medical treatment, and medical ethics. This sets the moral framework for a detailed discussion on reproductive control, biotechnical parenting, and the termination of fetal life.

I. ETHICAL NATURE OF THE ISSUES

> In Islam, ethics is inseparable from religion and is built entirely upon it. The Islamic mind knows no pair of contraries such as "religious-secular," "sacred-profane," "Church-State"; and Arabic, the religious language of Islam, has no words for them in its vocabulary.[1]

The universe, according to Islam, is teleological in the sense that it is based on the belief that the world was created for a divine purpose. Hence, "nature is equally a realm of ends where everything fulfills a purpose and thereby contributes to the prosperity and balance of all."[2]

The Qur'an affirms that man is the main "character" in this universe. He provides the *raison d'etre* for all that exists (14:33; 31:20; 35:39; 22:65). He is the vicegerent of Allah on earth (2:30). He was created with the primary purpose of serving Allah (51:56). Thus, Islam takes an optimistic view on the nature of man.

A. Man's Innocence

Man, the Qur'an affirms, is created by Allah pure and in the best of shape (95:4). He is inclined toward the good (100:8), and to serve his fellowmen, if properly guided (98:5). Therefore he is not in need of redemption but rather of guidance. He is not saved or doomed because of an accident of birth. The idea of original sin is absent in Islam and every individual is responsible for his own acts (52:16,21).

B. Man's Freedom

Strictly speaking only Allah is absolutely free, but to a certain degree man is also free. In the story of the Creation in the Qur'an, Adam was distinguished from all other creatures by his ability to think. Reason was given to man so that he may be in a position to freely accept the Law and obey Allah (SWT) or not do so at all. This freedom is a precious asset to man. In His Omnipotence, Allah (SWT) could have compelled man to obey the laws of nature, but then he would have been either an animal or an angel, but not man.[3] This accounts for man being also described in the Qur'an as rebellious (14:34), vain (96:6,7), and ungrateful (100:6). By his wrong doing, man falls short of perfect obedience, and is held accountable (4:85). The burden of responsibility and morality has been placed upon man as an opportunity to test his submission to Allah (SWT) so that he can be admitted into His presence.

C. Man's Social Responsibiity

Man is not to lead his life in isolation. He is part and parcel of the society. The Prophet (SAWS) warned that every person is a guardian and is responsible for those under his guardianship.[4] Moreover, the Prophet (SAWS) said that there is no monasticism in Islam.[5] Therefore man is prohibited from forsaking this world in order to gain salvation. Indeed, his very participation in socicty will determine his success or failure. For life in this world is his only chance to prepare for salvation in the next. Responsibility, in other words, demarcates the limits of man's freedom. Islam challenges man to search for and understand the patterns of Allah in nature and in himself so that he can respect and use the divine pattern in creation.

D. The *Shari'ah*

The *Shari'ah* literally stands for "the path" and serves to guide mankind by showing the criterion between right and wrong (Qur'an 25:1;2:256). Its injunctions are derived from both the Qur'an and *Hadith*, which express the commandments of Allah, (SWT).

The Qur'an is the record of the verbatim messages revealed to the Prophet Muhammad (SAWS). It is the primary source of the *Shari'ah*. It contains the bases of the Law as well as some explicit provisions of the Law.

The Qur'an comprehends all the general principles by which all religious and mundane matters are to be regulated, but not all of them are set out with equal clearness and details. The Qur'an affirms that the Prophet (SAWS) possessed not only the *Kitab*, i.e. the Qur'an, but also *hikmah*, i.e. wisdom. The sayings of the Prophet (SAWS) form a kind of commentary and supplement to the Qur'an in the event that there exists no explicit verse in the Qur'an on a particular issue. The Qur'an enjoins us to "obey Allah and His apostle" (3:32;8:24;4:59).

E. The Challenge of Islam

There is no doubt about the emphasis the Qur'an lays on the necessity of observing natural phenomena. It invites man to study creation as the handiwork of Allah (SWT) and to marvel at its beauty.

In the light of the teachings of the Qur'an the Prophet (SAWS) of Islam urged Muslims to seek knowledge and declared that its quest was incumbent upon his followers.[6] History bears witness to the fact that the exhortations of the Qur'an and the instruction of the Prophet (SAWS) did not fall on deaf ears. With the aim of understanding the design of their Creator that exists in nature, Muslims ventured into the scientific field and made break-throughs in most of its branches, such as, in mathematics, astronomy, physics, and optics.

Likewise, the injunctions of the Qur'an and *ahadith* of the Prophet (SAWS) pertaining to hygiene, dietary habits, and the necessity of upholding moderation in all walks of life, led the Muslims to the study of medicine. Abu Darda' reported that the Messenger of Allah said, "Allah has sent down both the disease and the cure, and He has appointed a cure for every disease...."[7] Moreover, there are many *ahadith* of the Prophet (SAWS) that concern illness and their cure. In fact, the *hadith* literature has a separate chapter entitled *al Tibb al Nabawi* or "Medicine of the Prophet." This gave the pursuit of the science of medicine a religious basis from the very beginning. History tells us that Muslims made great strides in the field of medical science. For example, the celebrated work of Ibn Sina (Avicenna d. 1037 A.C.), namely, *al Qanun*, served as the chief guide to medical science in Europe from the 12th century to the 17th century A.C.

It may be emphasized here that the motivating factor behind the Muslims' quest for knowledge in the scientific and medical fields was primarily to understand the creation of Allah (SWT) so as to be drawn closer to their Creator. Thus, it follows that it was never their aim to exploit nature selfishly, nor to dominate it as rivals to Allah (SWT), nor to exert control over life and death. Moreover, the concept that regulated the conduct of the Muslims in the pursuit of science was precisely the concept of *al-tawhid*, i.e., the Oneness of Allah (SWT). Ziauddin Sardar aptly stresses the importance of the concept of *al-tawhid*. He writes:

> It becomes an all embracing value when this unity is asserted in the unity of mankind, unity of man and nature, and the unity of knowledge and values. From *tawhid* emerges the concept of *khilafah*: that man is not independent of God but is responsible and accountable to God for his scientific and technological activities....[8]

Thus, the question of accountability necessarily implies that science and technology cannot be divorced from ethics. In Islam, however, ethics is not independent of the *Shari'ah*, i.e., Islamic law, but, rather, is part and parcel of it. In the West from the 17th century onwards, an atheistic tendency prevailed within the scientific field whereby the relevance of Allah (SWT) to the natural phenomena was deliberately rejected. Events in nature from then on have been explained in Euro-American civilization as the results of necessary causes that can never be other than what they are.

In the biomedical field there is a tendency to try to "conquer" death and to manipulate life through the process of genetic engineering. It is in this field that Muslims are confronted with a series of ethical issues that have legal connotations as well and must be explored.

The bifurcated Western civilization, which separates the sacred from the secular or denies it altogether, is in a dilemma. Muslims have an obligation to offer the guidance revealed in the Qur'an. Without this Divine Guidance, man may be governed by his own selfishness and arrogance. With it man has an ultimate basis for rational discourse in promoting the good and opposing the bad wherever it may be.

II. SCOPING THE PROBLEM

The scope of biomedical technology is immense and affects a wide range of issues:

- population control through the means of contraceptive devices, sterilization programs, etc;
- termination of life through the means of abortion, euthanasia, etc;

- prolongation of life through the means of organ transplantation, artificial organs, respirators, cardiac pacemakers, etc;
- sex pre-selection and sex-change operations;
- "improving" the quality of life through the means of genetic screening, genetic engineering, artificial insemination, and sperm banks;
- coping with fertility problems through the technique of test-tube ferilization, the use of "surrogate mothers," and ova banks, etc;
- experiments involving human-beings; and
- controlling behavior by physical means such as psychosurgery and psychotherapeutic drugs.

In view of the extensive nature and scope of biomedical science and technology, however, the author has chosen to restrict this book to three issues, namely, reproductive control, biotechnical parenting, and abortion. All of these issues Muslims may have to face, in one way or another, sometime in their lifetime. For example, biomedical technology has today devised countless ways of practicing birth-control by means of contraceptives. Could such modern techniques be acceptable within the Islamic tradition on the basis that it is reported that the Prophet (SAWS) did not stop his followers from practicing *coitus interruptus*, which was then the only viable way of practicing birth-control besides counting on the safe-period? Likewise, it may happen that the married couple may for one reason or another be unable to produce offspring. Biomedical technology today can determine the cause of infertility in either the male or female. It can even assist them in overcoming their infertility. Would resorting to any of the means by which the problem of infertility can be overcome be contrary to reliance on Allah (SWT), or tantamount to tampering with His *Sunan* ("Ways" or "natural laws")? Moreover, modern biomedical science has today invented ways and means by which it is possible to detect whether the fetus is afflicted with some sort of deformity. Could Muslims resort to abortion if such be the case?

All such issues are both "ethical" and "legal" within the Islamic tradition, because the *Shari'ah* encompasses both and does not distinguish between them. Islamic law is normative. Therefore in determining their "goodness" or "badness," certain specific legal terms will be used and need to be fully understood. Two levels of badness are:

- *Haram*: whatever is forbidden by having a clear proof from the Qur'an and *Hadith* (saying of the Prophet);
- *Makruh*: whatever is hated, improper, disliked, or undesirable, either by the Qur'an and or *Hadith* or by analogy and deduction.

This book, of course, is not the final answer to the above mentioned problems, but *insha'allah*, it may serve as one starting point for deeper study in the domain of biomedical science and as an impetus for future work on the relevance and impact of biomedical innovation in the lives of all persons and communities today and in the future.

Muslim scholars have not yet seriously probed the field of biomedical science. So far, only a few booklets have appeared within the Islamic world dealing with issues like organ transplantation. Family planning seems to be the only field with which Muslim scholars have attempted to deal extensively. Some have viewed such a movement as part of a colonialist conspiracy aimed at reducing their population. In dealing with family planning or birth-control as such, they have also touched superficially on the question of abortion. This book will deal with the issue of abortion separately, because abortion can in no way be considered part of contraception. So far as the techniques to overcome infertility are concerned, a few *fatawa* or legal opinions of the *Ulama* (religious scholars) are available.

The issues pertaining to reproductive control, biotechnical parenting, and abortion are dealt with under four parts. The first part serves as a background providing information needed to understand the attitude of Islam toward health care and medical treatment. It also touches on the subject of medical ethics. The second part deals with reproductive control. It is divided into four chapters (three, four, five, and six). The first chapter establishes the purpose of marriage. The second chapter analyses the views of the various schools of Islamic Law on the issue of contraception. The third chapter enumerates both the reversible and irreversible methods of contraception in order to determine which ones are acceptable and non-acceptable. The last chapter deals with birth control in history, examining the case of Pakistan.

The third part addresses the problem of infertility. It is divided into three chapters (seven, eight and nine). The first concerns itself with the references made to infertility by the Qur'an and the ways in which Muslims tried to overcome infertility problems before the recent breakthroughs in modern biomedical technology. Chapter eight analyzes the various ways by which biomedical technology attempts to solve the problem of infertility. The last chapter evaluates these biotechnical possibilities under the light of the Islamic teachings.

The fourth part of the book deals with abortion. It is divided into five chapters (ten, eleven, twelve, thirteen and fourteen). First, we deal with the definition of abortion and the sanctions laid down by the Qur'an and the *Hadith* against unjust termination of life. Then we analyze fetal development as viewed by science, the Qur'an, and the *Hadith*, as well as the rights of the fetus under Islamic law. The third chapter addresses various cases of unwanted pregnancies and the justification for abortion in each of them. Solutions for such unwanted pregnancies are highlighted and analyzed. The fourth chapter spells out instances where it would be legally acceptable to induce abortion, and presents the views of the classical Muslim physicians on the issue. The last chapter stipulates the Islamic punishment for feticide.

Biomedical issues have been dealt with extensively in the West. Such literature has been consulted for the understanding that it yields on the issues discussed in this book. The major source materials for this book, however, are four:

1) Basic works of *fiqh* (Islamic jurisprudence) such as *al Mughni* of Ibn Qudamah, *al Muwatta* of Imam Malik, *Hashiyah Radd al Muhtar* of Ibn Abidin, and *Kitab al Umm* of Imam al Shafi'i.
2) Basic works of *tafsir* (commentary on the Qur'an) by classical authorities, such as al Alusi, al Jassas, and Ibn Kathir. Such works provide substantial information on the direct reasons for the revelation of the Qur'anic verses (*asbab al nuzul*) and the significance or meaning of the verses.
3) Basic works on *al hadith* (the *Sunnah* or the Traditions of The Prophet) especially *al Sihah al Sittah* (the six canonical collections of *ahadith*).
4) Basic works of the classical Muslim physicians, such as *Kitab al Qanun fi al Tibb* of Ibn Sina and *Kitab al Hawi* of Muhammad Ibn Zakariyya al Razi.

PART ONE:

ISLAM AND HEALTH

CHAPTER I
PREVENTIVE AND CURATIVE MEDICINE

I. HEALTH PRESERVATION

The Qur'an is not a book of medicine but, rather, a book of guidance for mankind in both worldly and spiritual matters. Interestingly, however, Allah describes the Qur'an as "a guide and a healing to those who believe" (41:44). Man, the Qur'an informs us, is the crown of creation and the vicegerent of Allah (SWT) on earth (6:165). It thus follows that he is to be an active participant in this universe and certainly not a passive being. The world, so to say, is the arena wherein he has to prove his worth in the task assigned to him. He is a composite entity of body and soul and hence he is to take care of his body and ensure that it is healthy and strong so that he may actively participate both in multiplying the bounties of the earth and in the uplifting of his soul. This is why the Prophet (SAWS) remarked: "A strong believer is better and more liked by Allah (SWT) than a weak believer."[1] This *hadith* stresses the fact that Muslims should take good care of their health and always strive to remain in a healthy state. Health, it is to be noted, is a state of complete physical, mental, and social well-being and not merely the absence of disease and infirmity.

It is common knowledge that in order to ensure one's health, one should have a balanced diet, comprising wholesome food and drink, and avoid anything that may prove injurious to one's body. Towards that end, one should also maintain personal hygiene and take steps to assure mental health. The Qur'an provides sufficient guidance in these respects. It enjoins Muslims to partake of wholesome food: "O people! Eat of what is lawful and good on earth...." (2:168), and specifies the types of food that should be avoided: "He has forbidden you dead meat, and blood, and the flesh of swine, and that on which other than the name of Allah has been invoked" (2:173;16:115).

The prohibition against eating the flesh of swine is stipulated in both Judaism and Islam. In Leviticus 11:7-8, the flesh of swine is described as unclean and an order is given to shun it. From the injunctions of the Bible and the Qur'an against the eating of pork we can infer that the warning is primarily for health.

Intoxicating liquor is similarly proscribed. Muslims are prohibited to indulge in it, nay, or even to partake of it in a small quantity. The Qur'an testifies to the fact that there no doubt may be some benefit for man in it but cautions, saying: "They ask thee concerning intoxicants and gambling. Say: 'In both there is great evil and some benefit for man; but the evil they cause is greater than the benefit that they bring'" (2:219).

The evils of alcohol or liquor cannot be overemphasized. Today it poses a threat to the stability of society, even in the major industrialized countries of the world. This accounts for the establishment of "Alcoholics Anonymous" in such countries. The Qur'an speaks of its moral, social, and spiritual evils in the following manner: "O you who believe! Intoxicants...are an abomination of Satan's handiwork. Eschew such (abomination) that you may prosper. Satan's plan is to excite enmity and hatred among you, with intoxicants and gambling, and hinder you from the rememberance of Allah (SWT), and from prayer: will you not then abstain?" (5:93-4).

Besides the social evils that alcohol poses, it is today an accepted fact that it also has serious repercussions on one's health. For example, one's liver and kidneys can be affected by the constant onslaught of alcohol, which can even lead to the malfunctioning of one's excretory system. We have seen the founding of M.A.D.D. (Mothers Against Drunk Driving) in America. This action was prompted by the fact that a number of young Americans die as a result of drunk driving practically every holiday season. We are all aware of the effort to control this phenomenon. The mass media play an equally important role in this regard. American television cautions the citizens not to drink and drive. Moreover, it relays special programs designed to inform the public of the various drinks that are supposedly alcohol-free. These drinks can be used as substitutes for alcohol to be served to guests. This is to ensure their safe return home after the party. But, no emphasis at all is being given to urging the people to abstain totally from alcohol. As long as nothing is done toward this end, whatever is advocated as short-term solutions will not succeed in resolving the problem. The task may be colossal, but, it is not impossible. History tells us that when the injunction banning the intake of alcohol was revealed to the Prophet (SAWS), the city of Madinah witnessed the citizens pouring all their stocks of wine down the street drains. There was no hesitation on the part of the Muslims, no second thoughts. It was their strong faith in Allah (SWT) and their awareness of accountability before Him that made them succeed in getting rid of this scourge and refraining from it.

Insecurity and helplessness may lead to mental depression that can result in suicide. In order to counter this, the Qur'an teaches man to seek refuge in Allah: "...for, verily, in the remembrance of Allah (men's) hearts do find rest" (13:28). Moreover, the Qur'an declares all Muslims to be part and parcel of one large brotherhood, the ummah of Islam. The Prophet (SAWS) is reported to have said that the members of the ummah are like one body. If any of its parts is in pain then the rest of the body feels the pain.[2] This signifies that the Muslims are to take care of one another, to be concerned about the welfare of one another. The Qur'an teaches that most of the religious practices are to be performed or observed in congregation. No Muslim is, therefore, expected to feel insecure, helpless, lonely. Marriage has been enjoined upon men and women primarily so they will find peace, comfort, and tranquility with their respective mates. The institution of zakah is meant to assist the needy Muslims, so that no one need be mentally depressed in the face of economic hardships, or in the event of an emergency, such as the loss of one's job in time of recession.

The Qur'an exhorts Muslims to be conscious of personal hygiene. It enjoins upon Muslims the performance of ablution before engaging in the daily salah (obligatory prayers). It even stipulates the parts that should be washed during the process of ablution, namely, the face, the hands up to the elbows, the head, and the feet up to the ankles. Such parts are usually kept exposed. Moreover, the Qur'an makes it an obligation upon the married couple to take the ghusl (obligatory bath) after engaging in sexual intercourse (5:6).

Islam, like other religions, enjoins upon its adherents certain religious practices, but permits concessions for the sick. Imam Ibn Qayyim al Jawziyyah points out that the principles of medicine are three, namely, protection of health, getting rid of harmful things, and safeguarding against harm, and he asserts that concessions given to the sick are precisely for the sake of upholding these three principles. He elucidates this point by giving several examples. First, the verse pertaining to fasting: "But if any one is ill or on a journey, the prescribed period (should be made up) by (a similar number of days) later" (2:185), permits the sick and travelers to refrain from the compulsory fast in order to protect their health and strength. Second, the verse pertaining to Pilgrimage, "And if any of you is ill, or has an ailment in his scalp (necessitating shaving), (he should) in compensation either fast, or feed the poor, or offer sacrifice" (2:196), allows the sick or one who has a scalp problem requiring shaving, such as lice-infestion or scabies, to shave his head while still in the state of *ihram* (in the pilgrim garb) in order to treat the problem. From this it can be inferred that one should eliminate anything harmful. Third, in regard to safeguarding oneself against harm, the Qur'an says in the verse pertaining to ablution, "If you are ill, or on a journey, or one of you comes from offices of nature, or you have been in contact with women, and you find no water, then take for yourselves clean sand or earth, and rub therewith your faces and hands" (4:44). Thus, the sick, whose illness may be aggravated by use of water, are given permission to use sand or earth instead. This is an admonition to safeguard oneself from anything that might prove harmful to oneself either internally or externally.[3]

From the above, it is clear that Islam lays great emphasis on health so that man may be in a position to fulfill the duties assigned to him and excel in his role as the vicegerent of Allah (SWT) on earth. The Qur'an enjoins upon the Muslims certain dietary rules and exhorts them to be conscious of personal hygiene, and to engage in the remembrance of Allah (SWT) in ways that protect their health. By relaxing certain of its rules pertaining to religious practices, the Qur'an shows that it cares for the welfare of the sick. The concessions given to the sick support the three principles of medicine presented by Imam Ibn al Qayyim al Jawziyyah, namely, protecting health and both removing and avoiding all that is harmful to it.

II. RESTORATION OF HEALTH

Ibn Sina (Avicenna, 980-1036 A.C.) defined medicine – *al Tibb* – as the knowledge of the states of the human body in health and in any decline in health, that is, the purpose of medicine is to preserve health and to restore it whenever it has been lost.[4] Health is normally looked upon as a natural state of our lives, while illness or disease is a sort of unnatural condition that afflicts the human body and can be combated and cured by the use of proper medication. Illness or disease, no doubt, causes a lot of discomfort to the one afflicted, but in no way does any Muslim view such an affliction as a curse, wrath, or punishment of Allah (SWT). He is conditioned to view the discomfort of any sickness as a trial or ordeal which in reality brings about expiation of sins and may strengthen his character. It is reported that the Prophet (SAWS) said: "Never is a believer stricken with discomfort, hardship, illness, grief or even mental worry, except that his sins are expiated for him."[5]

At the same time, it should be borne in mind that Muslims are urged to seek medical attention whenever they fall sick. This is clear from portions of the Qur'an and *ahadith* of the Prophet (SAWS) classified under *al Tibb al Nabawi*. The importance of seeking medical attention or treatment is hinted by the Qur'anic verse that describes honey produced by the bees as having curative powers. It states: "...there issues from their bodies a drink of varying colours, wherein is a healing for men" (16:69).

Various compilations of *ahadith* include a chapter on *al Tibb al Nabawi* (Medicine of the Prophet), wherein are recorded the Prophet's sayings about illness, its treatment, and the sick. The importance of this literature is highlighted by Dr. Seyyed Hossein Nasr in the following manner: "Since all sayings of the Prophet are guideposts for the life of the devout Muslim, these latter sayings, even though they do not contain an explicit system of medicine, have played a major role in determining the general atmosphere in which Islamic medicine has come to be practiced. Their guidance has been followed over the centuries by every succeeding generation of

Muslims; they have determined many of the Muslims' dietary and hygienic habits. Moreover, 'The Medicine of the Prophet' became the first book to be studied by a medical student before he undertook the task of mastering the usual compendia of medical science. It has thus always played an important role in creating the frame of mind with which the Muslim physician has undertaken the study of medicine."[6]

The Prophet (SAWS) urged his followers to seek medical attention whenever they were unwell. The following incident is recorded in the *hadith* literature: "The Bedouin Arabs came to the Prophet (SAWS) and said, 'O Messenger of Allah, should we treat ourselves?' He replied, 'Yes, O servants of Allah, you must treat (yourselves): for verily, Allah has not created a disease without providing a cure for it, except for one disease.' They asked him: 'Which one is that?' He replied, 'Old age'."[7] Likewise, he is reported to have said, "For every disease there is a cure."[8] Moreover, the Prophet (SAWS) emphasized the importance of learning the art of medicine before attempting to practice it. He warned, "Whoever gives medical treatment and knows nothing about medicine is to be held culpable."[9]

Knowledge in any particular field enables one to discharge one's duty in the best manner possible. The physician has to be well-versed in his profession, for he has in his hands a human being as his patient and a mistake on his part, or ignorance, could expose the life of his patient to danger. This is why the Prophet (SAWS) advised his followers to seek medical assistance from the one who is knowledgeable in that particular field. It is reported by Jabir that when Ubayy bin Ka'b fell ill the Prophet (SAWS) sent a doctor to attend to him.[10] M.M. Sharif points out that the only known physician during the Prophet's time was al Harith ibn Kaladah, an Arab Jew who later embraced Islam.[11]

As far as contagious disease is concerned, the Prophet (SAWS) taught a very practical lesson. He said, "When plague is rampant in a locality do not go inside it... but if you are already inside then do not come out of it."[12] This saying prescribes the modern quarantine measures to isolate those who are contaminated by contagious diseases.

Since man is composed of body and soul, the Prophet (SAWS) pointed out two types of ailment, affecting each of two components separately or jointly. He remarked, "You have two cures at your disposal: Honey and the Qur'an."[13] From this saying it can be deduced that Muslims have the duty to pursue physical health as well as spiritual health. Today, it is accepted that honey has curative powers both internally when swallowed and externally when applied to wounds and sores. As far as the disease of the soul is concerned, Imam ibn Qayyim al Jawziyyah points out that the Qur'an refers to it as the disease of the heart, which may be either that of doubt and uncertainty or that of submission to one's sensual passion.

The Qur'an is the cure for such a disease.[14]

We have seen that the Qur'an declared alcoholic drinks to be *haram* (prohibited), which explains why practicing Muslims are teetotallers. The Prophet (SAWS) forbade the use of forbidden things as medicines, as is evident from the following:

Abu Dawud records in his *Sunan* that Abu al Darda reported that the Prophet (SAWS) said, "Allah created the disease and also the cure and for every disease He has provided a cure. So treat yourselves with medicines, but do not treat yourselves with prohibited things."[15] Imam al Bukhari records on the authority of Ibn Mas'ud (RA) that the Prophet (SAWS) said, "The Almighty Allah has not provided as treatment for you that which is prohibited."[16] Imam Muslim records that Tariq bin Suwayd al Ja'fiyyi (RA) asked the Prophet (SAWS) about *khamr* (intoxicating drink) and he forbade him from using it. When Tariq argued that he used it as medicine, the Prophet rejoined, "It is not a medicine but a malady."[17]

By urging his followers to seek medical attention, the Prophet (SAWS) wanted them to treat their sicknesses, whether of minor, major, epidemic, or non-epidemic consequences. Moreover, he did not restrict his followers to any particular method or way of alleviating their illnesses. This means that the Muslims may resort to an allopathic or homeopathic system or any other type of medical care. Hence, it necessarily follows that resorting to modern biomedical means is permissible for the Muslims. The Muslims may seek the assistance of any physician, Muslim or non-Muslim, and this can be deduced from the fact that the only known physician uring the Prophet's (SAWS) time was an Arab Jew, who must have attended to Muslim patients before finally accepting Islam.

Furthermore, the Prophet's (SAWS) saying that for every disease there is a cure impelled his followers to pursue studies in the field of medicine and make breakthroughs in most of its branches. It may have inspired them to build hospitals where the patients could be given proper medical care. History tells us that the first hospital built by the Muslims was in Damascus in 706 A.C.during the caliphate of Walid ibn 'Abd Malik. All treatment and care were dispensed free of charge.[18]

CHAPTER II
MEDICAL ETHICS

I. IN THE WEST

Medical ethics, during the last decade or so, has been much talked about, and today in most medical colleges in the United States it has been incorporated into the syllabus and is a very popular course. This chapter attempts to answer two questions: First, is medical ethics a new field altogether or does it have its roots in the origin of medicine as an independent science? Second, what guided Muslim physicians in this domain?

In reply to the first question, it is apt to note the observation of Dr. Ahmed Elkadi, one of the founder-members of the Islamic Medical Association of the United States and Canada, "For thousands of years, ethics has been recognized as an essential requirement in the making of a physician. The famous Oath of Hippocrates has stressed this fact and it still serves as a base line for all man-made codes of professional ethics."[1] Hence, it is evident that, during the past in European culture, though medical ethics as such was not talked about as it is today, it was upheld by each and every physician in view of the fact that they all had to take the Hippocratic Oath in order to be qualified in the field of medicine. Practically all the areas that are discussed in the domain of medical ethics today have already been laid down in the Hippocratic Oath. In order to illustrate this point, we shall consider at least three of the concepts included in modern medical ethics.

A. The Concept of Non-Maleficence

In layman's terms, non-maleficence encompasses avoidance of both intentional harm (i.e. injury) and intentional risk of harm. The example usually given for intentional harm is physical assault, while an example of the risk of harm is driving a vehicle at excessive speed. The salient difference between risk of harm and intentional harm may not be clearly demarcated. Beauchamp and Childress, however, state that, "under the prima facie duty of non-maleficence, intentional harm is prohibited except under very special conditions, such as self-defense, while risking harm is allowed under many conditions as long as the goals of the conduct are sufficiently important."[2] Medically speaking, the concept of non-maleficence would imply that the physician should not harm his patient intentionally, nor should he try to place the life of his patient in possible risk without justifying the probable benefits that may result thereby. In relation to this concept, the Hippocratic Oath, stipulates the following: "I will neither give a deadly drug to anybody if asked for it, nor will I make a suggestion to that effect."

B. The Concept of Beneficence

Beneficence may be defined as the "doing of good, active promotion of good, kindness and charity."[3] But what is important to be noted is that beneficence is meant to be regarded as a duty: duty to help others. In other words, the physician not only is expected to treat his patients and not harm them, but is expected to contribute to their health and welfare. The underlying factor in the patient-physician relationship is the understanding that the latter is expected to benefit the former. Interestingly, in the Hippocratic Oath, the physician makes a commitment to that effect: "I will come for the benefit of the sick" and "I will apply dietetic measures for the benefit of the sick according to my ability and judgment."

C. The Rule of Confidentiality

It cannot be denied that someone who discloses the secret of another person has in reality betrayed the trust given him. Such an act cannot be condoned. So far as the patient-physician relationship is concerned, the physician has the duty not to breach the confidentiality of his patient. Beauchamp and Childress maintain that he may breach the confidentiality of his patient only in the event that it is necessary to honor a strong conflicting duty.[4] In this regard, in the Hippocratic Oath, the physician makes the following commitment: "What I may see or hear in the course of the treatment or even outside of the treatment in regard to the life of man, which on no account one must spread abroad, I will keep to myself, holding such things shameful to be spoken about."

D. Subsequent Modifications of the Hippocratic Oath

In September 1948, the General Assembly of the World Medical Association, Geneva, Switzerland, adopted the "Physician's Oath," which was later on amended by the 22nd World Medical Assembly, Sydney, Australia, in August 1968.[5] It is evident that all the broad principles envisaged by the Hippocratic Oath have been maintained and slightly improved upon. The most striking difference between the two is that while the former (Hippocratic Oath) made the physician swear by the Greek gods and godesses that he would uphold the principles laid down in the Oath, the latter omits any reference to any Supreme Being. The modern contemporary physician takes the pledge on his own cognizance and initiative without expressing accountability to any form of Supreme Authority.

In January 1981, the International Organization of Islamic Medicine held its first conference in Kuwait under the auspices of the Kuwaiti Ministry of Health. The Muslim physicians from every nook and corner of the world expressed their dissatisfaction with both the Hippocratic Oath and its modified Geneva version. It is important that we understand why they took such a stand. The most fundamental teaching in Islam is the doctrine of Oneness of Allah (*al tawhid*), which is expressed in the *shahadah* or confession of Islamic faith. This confession states that "there is no god but God." This implies that Allah (SWT) is the Eternal, the Ultimate, the Creator, the Transcendent. Nothing is like unto Him. He remains forever absolutely unique and without rivals (i.e. partners or associates). It was, therefore, natural that they could not accept the clause in the Hippocratic Oath whereby reference is made to the multiplicity of gods and allegiance is made to them in upholding the principles. Likewise, they could not accept the Geneva version in view of the fact that invocation of the deity (Allah) is totally absent. It ought to be remembered that Allah (SWT) occupies the central position in every Muslim environment and in every Muslim thought. A Muslim does not embark upon any action without invoking the name of Allah (SWT). The presence of Allah (SWT) fills the devout Muslim's consciousness at all times. He is aware of his accountability before Him. Thus, the Islamic Conference adopted the "Oath of the Muslim Doctor," wherein the name of Allah (SWT) has been incorporated and the pledge is made in His Name that the physician would uphold its principles.[6]

We have to admit that what is common in all of the three versions of the Oath is that the principles envisaged in them are the same and that these principles were primarily intended to assist the physician to achieve a high standard of moral conduct. These principles are indeed vital in determining the physician's conduct vis-a-vis his patients, colleagues, members of their profession, and the public in general.

II. IN ISLAM

Dr. Abdul Hamid observes: "When we scan the Arabic literature for material on medical ethics, we are faced with the peculiar dilemma that the great work of Ibn Sina, *Al Qunan fi al Tibb*, which totals five volumes, extends over 2000 pages, and contains a million words, is completely silent on "medical ethics."[7] But, we must point out that the classical Muslim physicians like Ibn Sina did not speak on medical ethics as such because in their minds medical ethics was in no way divorced from the broad ethical teachings of the Qur'an and *Sunnah* of the Prophet (SAWS). In his last sermon, the Prophet (SAWS) highlighted the importance of these two sources in the following manner: "I leave behind two things; if you hold fast to them you shall never go astray: the Book of Allah and my *Sunnah*."[8]

Muslims, whatever their professions may be, regard themselves as Muslims first; that is, they perceive themselves as commissioned or conscripted by Allah (SWT) to reflect Islamic values in the pursuit of their vocations. These values are embodied in the Qur'an and *Sunnah*. Thus, these two sources of Islamic Ethịcs serve as adequate guidance for the patient in his affliction and for the doctor in his practice.

Nizami Arudi of Samarkand (sixth century A.H./twelfth century A.C.) describes the qualities of the Muslim physician in the ollowing terms: "The physician should be of tender disposition and wise nature, excelling in acumen, this being a nimbleness of mind in forming correct views, that is to say, a rapid transition from the unknown to the known. And no physician can be of tender disposition if he fails to recognize the nobility of the human soul; nor of wise nature unless he is acquainted with logic, nor can he excel in acumen unless he is strengthened by the aid of Allah; and if he is not acute in conjecture he will not arrive at a correct understanding of any ailment"...[9] In other words, what was expected of a Muslim doctor was to combine within himself scientific acumen and high moral qualities. Scientific acumen can be achieved only if one is prepared to engage oneself continuously in the quest of knowledge and is willing to carry out research in one's field. Both the Qur'an and *Sunnah* of the Prophet (SAWS) exhort Muslims to continue to pursue knowledge. For example, the Qur'an admonishes the Muslims to pray thus: "O my lord! Advance me in knowledge" (20:114). The Prophet (SAWS) exhorted his followers to make the quest of knowledge a permanent process of their lives, declaring: "The quest of knowledge is incumbent upon every Muslim male or female."[10]

Doctors are all the same as far as the training they get in the field of medicine, but a Muslim doctor is different from a non-Muslim doctor in his attitude toward death, toward his patients, and toward his role as healer, in view of the fact that he is expected to regulate his conduct in accordance with the teachings of the Qur'an and *Sunnah*. It may be apt to note here that the *hukama* (sing. *hakim*) or wise men, who were versed in both philosophy and medicine, did not restrict themselves to the pathological prognosis of their patients' diseases but were also much concerned about their spiritual, social, and psychological well-being.

Some characteristics which may distinguish Muslim from non-Muslim physicians are the following:

A. The Inevitability of Death

The Qur'an teaches that Allah (SWT) who is the Giver of life is also the One who causes death. It states: "It is He who created death and life, that He may try which of you is best in deed" (67:2). Moreover, it states that death is an inevitable consequence over which no one has control: "nor can they control death nor life nor resurrection" (25:3). Referring to the inevitability of death, Ibn Sina states: "It should be remembered that knowledge of health preservation helps neither in avoiding death nor in escaping from external afflictions. It also does not provide the means of extending life indefinitely."[11]

Unfortunately there is some tendency in advanced technological countries to deny the inevitability of death, for to accept it as inevitable would be tantamount to accepting the defeat of man by nature. Hence, in such countries, men are engaging in several projects with the aim of combating death. A major problem of people in such countries is that they are part of a death-denying culture. Whatever discoveries are made in the field of biomedical science are made with the primary aim of "conquering" death. For example, when Barney Clark, the 61 year old retired dentist who in 1982 was the recipient of the first artificial heart, died, television announced his death but added that the artificial heart (the invention of man) was still pumping.

This in no way suggests that the Muslim physician is against biomedical technology when it attempts to sustain life by placing a patient on a respirator or other such devices. Indeed, to endeavour to save life is a noble task, as the Qur'an states: "And whoever saves the life of a human being, it is as if he has saved the life of all mankind...." (5:32).

Thus, the author does not agree with David Suzuki who seems to criticize any heroic attempt toward sustaining life.[12] Consider attempts made to sustain the life of Barney Clark by means of a permanent artificial heart; or of David – the boy in the bubble – who lived out his short life encased in a sterile plastic space in a Houston hospital room because he was born without the capacity to produce antibodies. As a final example, Baby Fae was born with a defective heart and received a baboon's heart at California's Lome Linda University Medical Center. These cases were justified in the sense that they were attempts to save the lives of these people. Not to have attempted to do anything for them would conflict with the Qur'anic injunction on the importance of saving human lives (5:32). But, we must condemn any belief that such attempts do in fact conquer death. Islam teaches that death is inevitable and will occur only at the time decreed for it by Allah (SWT). The Qur'an states: "And for all people a term has been set. And when the end of the term approaches, they can neither delay it by a single moment, nor can they hasten it" (10:49).

B. Respect for Patients

The physician's respect for his patients encompasses a number of responsibilities toward them. He should use the appropriate words in conversing with them. The Qur'an describes the successful physicians and other professionals as people who "have been guided (in this life) to the purest of speech"(22:24). Furthermore, the physician should not disclose the secrets and feelings of his patients in view of the fact that the Qur'an describes the believers as those, "who faithfully observe their trusts and their covenants" (23:8). If he discovers, however, that his patients are suffering from venereal disease as a result of sexual licence, his duty would be not merely to cure them, but to guide them toward chastity, purity, and self-restraint. Moreover, the physician should never sexually abuse his patients if they be of the opposite sex. Dr. Elkadi suggests that it would be advisable that the physician examine patients of the opposite sex in the presence of a third person whenever feasible, for that could guard against any attempt leading toward abuse of one's patients sexually.[13]

Likewise, the physician should not overcharge his patients for services rendered to them. He should be considerate to those who may not be in a position to pay him for his services. The following Qur'anic verse should guide him in this respect: "And they feed, for the love of Allah, the indigent, the orphan, the captive, (saying), 'We feed you for the sake of Allah alone: no reward do we desire from you, nor thanks'" (76:8-9).

C. Reliance upon Allah as the Ultimate Healer

The physician, no doubt, can play an instrumental role in healing his patients from disease by prescribing to them medicine or surgery. But it would make a lot of difference if he believes that Allah (SWT) is the Ultimate Healer. In the event that a patient dies while under his care, his reliance on Allah (SWT) as the Ultimate Healer would assist him in overcoming the feeling of guilt, which most doctors feel. But it should be borne in mind that such belief in Allah (SWT) as the Ultimate Healer does not absolve any doctor of any mistake in diagnosis or treatment that results in the death of his patient. Ibn Rushd states that the Muslim jurists unanimously hold a doctor responsible for any mistake that he may commit.[14]

Thus, medical ethics, though much talked about today, is as old as medicine itself. Although the Hippocratic Oath has served as the basic guide for physicians, Muslim physicians derive ample guidance from the broad teachings of the Qur'an and sayings of the Prophet (SAWS), which determine their attitudes toward their profession and their patients.

It is appropriate here to point out that the first Islamic Medical Conference held in Kuwait in January, 1981, drafted the "Islamic Code of Medical Ethics" from the Qur'anic and Prophetic teachings, which is today available in booklet form in both the Arabic and English languages.[15] These two original sources of Islamic medical ethics can and should serve as guideposts to Muslim physicians the world over.

PART TWO:
REPRODUCTIVE CONTROL

CHAPTER III
THE PURPOSE OF MARRIAGE

Before dealing with the attitude of Islam toward reproductive control, we must consider the purpose of marriage. Reproductive control can in no way be viewed in isolation, for it is common experience that when a man and a woman enter in matrimony the natural result of that union is the production of offspring, whereas reproductive control is the act of keeping procreation in check. The Qur'an exhorts Muslims to marry, stating: "Marry those among you who are single, or the pious among your slaves...." (24:32).

This means that marriage is a desirable institution and a necessity. The Prophet (SAWS) is reported to have remarked that there is no celibacy in Islam. To enter into matrimony necessarily implies the fulfilment of the *Sunnah* (practice of The Prophet).[1]

Illicit sexual relations reflect irresponsibility and are regarded as a heinous crime in Islam. It is precisely to prevent such a crime that the Prophet (SAWS) admonished his followers to marry.[2] The institution of marriage was created by Allah (SWT) and therefore it is morally good to engage in sex with one's lawful wife. Sex is a natural desire like food and drink, growth and death.[3] The institution of marriage legitimizes the fulfilment of this desire, which is otherwise forbidden, and fosters equally important other purposes, namely, the happiness of the person and the well being of the community.

Procreation of the human species may be considered one of the most important aspects of marriage in view of the fact that men are regarded by the Qur'an to be the vicegerents of Allah (SWT) on earth. This means that men have been entrusted to act on this earth on behalf of Allah (SWT) in accordance with the Law (2:29-38). Moreover, everything that is to be found in the cosmos is for the benefit of mankind. Humans are the main characters in creation, and it is for their sake that a number of Prophets (AS) appeared in different ages to guide them with promises of heavenly life if successful and an abode in hell if unsuccessful.

This understanding may have prompted Mawdudi to regard procreation as the foremost purpose of marriage. He states, "Biologically man is a tiller and woman a tilth and the foremost purpose of the inter-relationship between the two is the procreation of the human race."[4] This position is not tenable. The Qur'an maintains that the relationship between husband and wife should be based on mutual love, cooperation, and compassion. The husband and wife ought to console each other, find tranquility with each other, and be a source of joy, happiness, and fulfilment for each other.

Moreover, the love between the husband and wife is not meant to be of a momentary nature but, rather, a life-long bond. If this cannot be realized, then Islam makes provision for divorce. Marriage in Islam, unlike in Christianity, is considered to be a contract, not a sacrament. That is why there is leniency for divorce, after a prescribed process of reconciliation, in the event that things do not work out between the two contracting persons. By intermarrying and procreating, as well as by living together, human beings do in fact fulfil the purpose of Allah (SWT). Love generated between the husband and wife soon develops into a love for the offspring and eventually that love is transcended to encompass all of Allah's creatures.

Family life serves to protect people from loneliness. It teaches one to be responsible, to cherish and love the members of the family, to be concerned for one another, and to care and share. For the fulfilment of these ends Islam strongly maintains that the family should be of an extended nature. Within the Islamic framework, the nuclear family would not and could never be the norm. The Qur'an directs Muslims to look after their elderly parents as well as other relatives. Thus, the very existence of nursing homes for senior citizens is virtually inconceivable within a truely Islamic environment.

It is clear from the above that the purpose of marriage in Islam is multi-dimensional. It is regarded as a commendable act to procreate the species and a means to curb illicit sexual relations, but equally as a bond of mutual love between the husband and wife and as the basic unit of every human community.

It seems equally un-Islamic to argue, as does Mohammad Saleem,[5] that, since procreation is not the sole purpose of marriage, family planning should be given a "carte blanche." A union between a husband and wife that does not result in offspring causes unhappiness. Procreation assures that the beautiful goals of the family life, enumerated above, can be realized. Reproductive control signifies the direct opposite. Thus, the question of its legality arises.

CHAPTER IV
CONTRACEPTION

Contraception may be defined as any measure undertaken to avoid the possibility of giving birth to children. Hence, such a measure necessarily implies the non-fulfillment of one of the purposes of marriage, namely, procreation of the human species. This chapter addresses, first, the issue whether contraception is permitted in Islam. We will examine the sources of decision. Second, we will examine the reasons given to justify contraception.

I. ISLAMIC SOURCES

The basic sources assessing the morality of contraception in Islamic law are the Qur'an, *ahadith*, and the use of *ijtihad* in analogy. The Qur'an, which is the verbatim word of Allah (SWT), does not make any categorical statement either in favour of or against contraception as such.

There may be a weak analogy in its condemnation of infanticide, which was generally restricted to female infants and in vogue in pre-Islamic Arabia. For example, it states: "Kill not your children for fear of want: We shall provide sustenance for them as well as for you. Verily killing them is a great sin" (17:31). And likewise it states: "Kill not your children on a plea of want; We provide sustenance for you and for them" (6:151).

Some scholars like Mawdudi reflected on these verses and came to the conclusion that if procreation is stopped due to fear of scarcity of resources and food, then it would be tantamount to the crime of infanticide.[1] This position is far-fetched. These verses were revealed in order to put an end to the inhuman practice of female infanticide, a custom that prevailed in pre-Islamic Arabia. Girls were considered a liability to the family. Hence, the moment they were born, they were buried alive. Although there is no doubt that Islam prohibited or eliminated this practice, no deduction may be made from this prohibition to condemn contraception. The latter is by nature different from infanticide. Infanticide is the actual killing of an already existing child, whereas contraception involves no killing and the supposed "child" does not yet exist. It is a common fact that during the process of reproduction only one sperm finally succeeds in fertilizing the ovum. Does this mean that all the other countless sperms that eventually die are dead children?

Others analogize from the Qur'anic support of natural fertility control. The Qur'an encourages mothers to nurse their children: "The mothers shall give suck to their offspring for two whole years" (2:233). This has led some scholars like Dr. 'Abdel R. Omran to infer that this verse implies a minimal spacing period of thirty-three months between children: nine months for pregnancy and twenty-four for lactation. During this period the chance of pregnancy is reduced by the physiological effects of lactation, which controls fertility in a natural manner.[2]

Imam Abu Bakr al Jassas, the illustrious Hanafi scholar, in his commentary on the Qur'an, states that Imam Abu Hanifah held that the Qur'anic verse, "Your wives are a tilth unto you; so approach your tilth when or how you will" (2:223), means that you have the option of practicing *'azl* (*coitus interruptus*) with your wife if you so desire.[3]

We can only conclude from the Qur'anic verses on nursing and intercourse that the Qur'an is silent on contraception, which means that we must look for guidance in the *ahadith* or inspired words and practice of the Prophet Muhammad (SAWS).

If jurists cannot judge the morality of acts on the basis of guidance in an explicit Qur'anic statement applicable to the issue in question, they turn to the *Hadith* or *Sunnah* of the Prophet (SAWS), which categorizes all acts in a spectrum of desirability. The five categories are:

1) *Halal*, i.e., good and encouraged without restriction;
2) *Mandub*, i.e., desirable or recommended in general;
3) *Mubah*, i.e., permissible, neither encouraged nor discouraged;
4) *Makruh*, i.e., generally blameworthy, hated, improper, or undesirable; and
5) *Haram*, i.e., bad by nature, absolutely unlawful.

The contraceptive method that was practiced during the lifetime of the Prophet (SAWS) is known as *al'azl*. *Al'azl* is derived from the Arabic verb *'azala*, which literally means to put apart, set aside, to remove or separate.[4] Technically speaking, "it is used to describe the process of withdrawal by the man at the time of emission to prevent insemination of the ovum."[5]

Imam al Shawkani has compiled all the *ahadith* dealing with *'azl* in his celebrated work "*Nayl al Awtar*" of which some are quoted below:[6]

1) Jabir narrates, "We used to practice *'azl* (coitus interruptus) in the Prophet's (SAWS) lifetime while the Qur'an was being revealed." Another version of the same *hadith* reads, "We used to practise *'azl* during the Prophet's lifetime and he was informed about this and he did not forbid us."
2) Jabir (RA) narrates, "A man come to the Prophet (SAWS) and said,

'I have a slave-girl, and we need her as a servant and around the palm groves. I have sex with her, but I am afraid of her becoming pregnant.' The Prophet said, 'Practice *'azl* with her if you so wish, for she will receive what has been predetermined for her'."

3) Abu Sa'id (RA) narrates, "The Jews say that *'azl* is minor infanticide, so the Prophet (SAWS) said, 'The Jews are wrong; for if Allah wanted to create something, no one can divert Him'."
4) 'Umar ibn al Khattab (RA) narrates, "The Prophet (SAWS) forbade the practice of *'azl* with a free woman except with her permission."
5) Judhamah bint Wahb (RA) narrates, "I was there when the Prophet (SAWS) was with a group of people when he said, 'I was about to prohibit the *ghila* (the act of engaging in sexual intercourse with a woman in lactation), but I observed the Byzantines and the Persians, and saw them do it, and their children were not harmed.' Then they asked him about *'azl* and the Prophet said, 'It is minor infanticide'."

Now, the first three *ahadith*, mentioned above, clearly reveal that the Prophet (SAWS) was aware of the practice of *coitus interruptus* among the people during his lifetime and did not stop them from it. But, *hadith* no.4 above, stipulates that the permission of one's wife (free woman) should be sought before engaging in this practice. *Hadith* no.2 and 3 make it clear that whoever is destined to be created will be by Allah's (SWT) infinite power and even practicing *coitus interruptus* would not frustrate Allah's plan. *Hadith* no. 5 of Judhamah, however, poses a problem. In it, the Prophet (SAWS) likens *'azl* to minor infanticide while in *hadith* no.3 he belies the Jews for holding *'azl* to be akin to minor infanticide. Muslim scholars have attempted to explain the apparent contradiction in these two *ahadith* in several ways. We shall here cite the survey by Imam Ibn Hajar in this respect. In his famous commentary on Sahih al Bukhari, *Fath al Bari*, Ibn Hajar discussed the issue in depth. First, he points out that some scholars regard the *hadith* narrated by Judhamah as weak (*da'if*) in view of the fact that it contradicts a number of *ahadith* (on that issue), and he notes that these scholars question how it could be possible for the Prophet (SAWS) to condemn the Jewish teachings and then elsewhere teach the same thing.[7]

Secondly, Ibn Hajar says that other scholars hold the *hadith* of Judhamah as abrogated. In that regard, he quotes the view expressed by al Tahawi who says that it is quite possible that the *hadith* of Judhamah reflects what was agreed upon earlier in conformity with the opinion of the People of the Book (Jews and Christians). The Prophet (SAWS), he observes, loved to comply with the views of the People of the Book in any matter not covered by revelation to him. But then Allah (SWT) inspired him with specific knowledge in this regard, so he contradicted what the Jews were saying. Ibn Hajar mentions that Ibn Rushd, and later on Ibn

Arabi in commenting on the view of al Tahawi, asserted that the Prophet (SAWS) never tried to follow the Jews.

Thirdly, Ibn Hajar noted that Ibn Hazm, the strict Spanish scholar, was more inclined to abide by the *hadith* of Judhamah. He considered that this *hadith* abrogated all the previous *ahadith* allowing the practice of *coitus interruptus*.

Finally, Ibn Hajar argued in support of Ibn Qayyim al Jawziyyah that the Jews were contradicted because they held that pregnancy could not occur if *'azl* was practiced, which means that they ranked it with infanticide in preventing progeny. The Jews were corrected and informed that *'azl* does not necessarily prevent pregnancy if Allah (SWT) so wills it to happen, and if Allah (SWT) does not will creation then *'azl* cannot be regarded as true infanticide. But in the *hadith* of Judhamah, *'azl* has been termed "minor infanticide" because the man who practices *'azl* is trying absolutely to prevent pregnancy, so his intention is the same as infanticide. The difference between the two is that infanticide is a direct and deliberate act. In it, both the intention and the action are combined, whereas *'azl* is restricted to intention only (that of not having any more dependants). Accordingly, it was termed a minor form of infanticide.

Relying on Ibn Qayyim's above reasoning (*ijtihad*), we see no clear contradiction between hadith no. 3 and no. 5. Moreover, in the latter hadith of Judhamah there is no explicit categorical statement against the practice of *'azl* as being *haram*. We can infer only that the Prophet (SAWS) was hinting that such a practice is *makruh* or undesirable but not absolutely prohibited. As Imam al Ghazali explains: "The remark 'it is minor infanticide' may be like his remark about 'minor disbelief' (*shirk khafi* or hidden or indirect shirk) which may be undesirable (*makruh*) but not illegal."[8]

The use of analogy (*qiyas*) from the Qur'an and *hadith* has produced general agreement among all of the major schools of law on contraception. They hold *'azl* (*coitus interruptus*) to be a permissible but blameworthy (i.e., *makruh*) practice, because the act by its nature deprives women the right to experience sexual fulfillment and to have children.[9] Imam Abu Hamid al Ghazali explains why *'azl* is considered to be *makruh* (undesirable or improper) in the following manner : "The custom of *'azl* is lawful but it is not commendable for the reason that the merits of depositing the semen in the uterus are given up. For instance, it is *makruh* or not desirable or not commendable if a person sits idle in a mosque without remembering Allah (SWT). The concept is that not using a thing for which it is intended is *makruh*. There is virtue in producing a child but this is given up in *'azl*."[10]

Hanafi School

Imam al Kasani, a scholar of this school states that it is undesirable (*makruh*) for the husband to practice *'azl* with his wife (free woman) without her permission, because the intercourse that results in ejaculation is the cause for procreation, and she has the right to have children. *'Azl* leads to the non-procreation of the child and thus would negate her right. But if *'azl* is practiced with her approval then it is not improper, for she has consented to the temporary loss of her right.[11]

Maliki School

Imam Malik bin Anas, the author or compiler of *al Muwatta*, the basic text of this school, says that a man has no right to practice *'azl* with his wife (free woman) without her consent.[12]

Shafi'i School

Imam al Nawawi, a scholar of this school, explains that al *'azl* is to engage in sexual intercourse, but prior to ejaculation (the man) removes (his penis) and allows the ejaculation to take place outside the vagina. He states that "this act is *makruh* (undesirable or not commendable), in any condition, whether the woman consents or not....But if his wife (the free woman) consents to it then it is not haram (forbidden) and if she does not give her consent, there are two opinions and the correct opinion is that it is not *haram* (forbidden)."[13]

Hanbali School

Ibn Qudamah, a jurist of this school, says that practicing *'azl* without any reason is *makruh* (undesirable or improper) but it is not *haram* (forbidden).... *'Azl* should not be practiced with a free woman without her consent.[14]

Ja'fari School

This school, like the four above-mentioned schools, stipulates that *'azl* (*coitus interruptus*) with a free woman is licit only with her specific permission but allows for the establishment of the woman's general consent as a precondition in the marriage contract.[15]

Thus, the insistence on the wife's permission, as stated above, is to ensure her right to have children and her right to maximum pleasure in the act of intercourse.

II. REASONS FOR CONTRACEPTION

A *hadith* of the Prophet (SAWS) states that "actions are judged by intentions."[16] We have seen that *'azl* is regarded as an undesirable (*makruh*) practice. But in cases where the life of the mother would be threatened if she became pregnant, or if repeated pregnancies would weaken her body, then practicing *'azl* would be necessary, and the juristic principle of the "rule of necessity" (*ḍarura*) would sanction the practice in order to save the life of the woman or her health. The principle of "necessity" merely means that the goal (*maqsid*) of life in a given case has higher priority than the goal of sustaining family and community (*nasl*), which are two of the half dozen highest purposes or values in Islamic law. It is a known fact, for example, that eating the flesh of dead animals is *haram* (forbidden). But in the event of possible starvation and the total absence of food, eating it would become not only legitimate, but a necessary duty to save one's life. The principle involved here is the intention of the overall *corpus* of Islamic law, which does not permit the violation of any divine ordinance. A number of Qur'anic verses may be cited to support the "rule of necessity" and two of them will be sufficient for our purpose: "Allah desires for you ease; He desires no hardship for you" (2:185); "He has not laid upon you in religion any hardship" (22:78).

Among the traditional scholars, the one who has dealt with the question of the acceptable reasons for one to practice *'azl* is the illustrious scholar, Imam al Ghazali (d. 1111 A.C.). In his famous *Ihya*, he states that the practicing of *'azl* would be justified if it were done for the sake of protecting the wife's life from the risk of child-birth, or if one fears excessive hardship (*kathrah al haraj*) because of too much child-bearing, or in case of genuine financial difficulty.[17]

Turning to recent times, among the modern scholars who have carefully considered the genuine reasons for contraception is Shaykh Ahmad al Sharabassi of Egypt.[18] He states that contraception is valid in the following four circumstances:

1) When the wife needs a chance to rest between pregnancies.
2) If either or both partners have a disease (genetic defect) that can be transmitted.
3) When the woman's health is threatened. For instance, if a woman is already suckling an infant, it would be harmful both for herself and her child if she became pregnant.
4) If the husband's finances are insufficient to support more children.

Of the acceptable reasons put forth by al Ghazali and Shaykh al Sharabassi the ones relating to the life and health of the wife are certainly tenable. In these cases, the juristic rule of necessity, invoking the goal of life (*haqq al hayah*) would make the use of contraceptive devices an obligation.

On the other hand, the argument of financial problems will not hold weight. This is so because within an Islamic society, the *Bait al Mal* would take care of the Muslims in financial difficulties. Within a Muslim society without an Islamic government or even in a non-Muslim country, the institution of *zakah* (poor due) should be properly managed to benefit the needy Muslims. Imam al Ghazali's consideration of excessive child-bearing, without any threat to life or health, may also not hold weight. For in Islam emphasis is placed on an extended family. There are always other members of the family around to give a helping hand.

Shaykh al Sharabassi's second reason refers to preventing the birth of children with genetic diseases. Its validity can be substantiated by genetic screening to establish that one or both of the prospective parents are carriers of certain genetic diseases and that there exists a strong probability of their begetting a deformed child. Taking such precautionary steps by means of contraception to prevent such birth can in no way be comparable to the actual killing of deformed fetuses through the act of abortion after fertilization has already taken place.

Summing up, it can be said that the Qur'an does not make any explicit reference to contraception as such, but the *ahadith* are clear on the issue. It is evident from the *sunnah* of the Prophet (SAWS) that Muslims may practice birth control or contraception, especially in the form of *'azl*. Nevertheless the five schools have ruled that *'azl* is *makruh* (undesirable or improper). The rationales generally used to justify contraception are: a threat to the life or health of the wife, the non-threatening burden of frequent child-bearing, the chance of transmitting a genetic defect, and financial stringency. These are given in descending order of legitimacy. The present author concludes that only the first rationale, a physical threat to the wife, is unquestionably sound.

CHAPTER V
CONTRACEPTIVE METHODS

In the previous chapter we have seen that the only type or method of contraception that was known and practiced during the lifetime of the Prophet (SAWS) was *'azl* or *coitus interruptus*.

Modern biomedical sciences have succeeded in devising new techniques or methods of contraception, and more research is being carried out to perfect the already existing means of contraception. Such methods may be categorized under reversible and irreversible methods.

Before dealing with them, it is appropriate to investigate whether Muslim jurists sanction female use of contraceptives. The permissibility of female use of contraceptives is sometimes treated as a distinct issue. As early as the 14th century after Christ, Ibn Taymiyyah (d. 1328 A.C.), the renowned Hanbali theologian and jurisconsult, was asked about female use of contraceptive devices. Both the question and reply in this regard have been recorded in his "*Fatawa*"[1] as follows:

Question: Is it lawful (*halal*), or permissible (*ja'iz*), for a woman to insert a "medicine" at the time of sexual intercourse so as to prevent the sperm from reaching the uterus? And if that "medicine" stays inside her after intercourse and it is not removed, is it permissible for her to offer her obligatory ritual of *Salah* and engage in fasting (*Sawm*) after taking the obligatory bath (*ghusl*) or not?

Answer: As regards her offering the obligatory *Salah* and engaging in fasting they are both valid in spite of the fact that "medicine" remains inside her. But as regards the permissibility (of using such a medicine) there is a difference of opinion among the *'Ulama* (scholars) and it would be more prudent not to use it; and Allah knows best.

Ibn Taymiyyah in no way condemned the practice but advised that one should be cautious in using such "medicine" and that it would be preferable that the woman not use it. Perhaps he was referring to the harm that "medicine" could do to the health of the woman.

The Hanafi jurist, Ibn Nujaym (d. 1563 A.C.), on the other hand, maintained that the "sealing of the opening of the uterus" by analogy to the classical opinion on coitus interruptus (*'azl*) should be subject to the husband's consent.[2]

I. Reversible Methods

Reversible methods are not of a permanent nature. The following ten methods fall in this category:

1) Douche
2) Rhythm method
3) Withdrawal (*'azl*)
4) Spermicides only (suppositories, foaming tablets, etc.)
5) Condom (sheath)
6) Diaphragm (cap)
7) Intra-uterine device (I.U.D.: e.g., loop, coil, etc.)
8) Progestogen - pill only
9) Progestogen injection.
10) The Pill

The principle involved in the third method above is to prevent the sperm from reaching the uterus and thus frustrating the possibility of the fertilization of the ovum. All the other methods have the same aim, so by analogy there would be no difficulty in accepting such methods.

There may be some problem with devices that prevent implantation, not fertilization, such as the IUD. The "South African Family Medical Adviser" points out the following: "Pregnancy can occasionally occur even with the device in place, and if it does, there is a greater risk of abortion between the fourth and sixth months, and an increased chance of the pregnancy being ectopic (at a site outside the womb)."[3] Since the IUD may result in the woman aborting the fetus if she does become pregnant, the very use of IUD becomes questionable.

Imam al Ghazali is of the opinion that fertilization is the essential factor and disturbing it would be a crime.[4] This would make questionable the use also of any methods against fertilization. Since the use of all contraceptive objects is considered *makruh* (undesirable, improper) within Islamic law and not *haram* (forbidden), involving ourselves unnecessarily in technicalities would only complicate matters. In determining what type of contraceptive method to use, every woman therefore should avoid whatever ones might threaten to harm her health.

II. Irreversible Methods

Irreversible methods are permanent in nature. The following methods be-

long to this category:
1) Vasectomy
2) Tubal ligation
3) Hysterectomy

All the above methods produce sterility and involve surgical intervention. If a woman chooses tubal ligation or hysterectomy as a method of contraception, and a man chooses vasectomy, then both the man and woman would be rendered permanently incapable of biological reproduction. Total hysterectomy, i.e., the removal of the entire uterus, is not chosen by most women as a method to avoid conception. Such a measure involves major surgical procedure and is a risky affair.[5]

It may be argued that tubal ligation is not a permanent measure and if a woman so desires later on to bear children the fallopian tubes can be "untied" or "joined" again. But it is worth noting that Robert H. Glass, M.D., and Ronald J. Ericsson, Ph.D., have remarked in this regard, "Tubal sterilization is often called 'tying the tubes,' and some who desire reversal of the sterilization are shocked to discover that repair of the tubes requires significantly more than just untying a knot. In fact, sterilization involves the removal or destruction by cauterization (burning) of a portion of the tube.... The chances for successfully rejoining the severed segments of each tube (tubal reanastomosis) depend, to some extent, on the technique used to do the sterilization."[6]

Likewise, it may be argued that vasectomy also is reversible, though risky, and that categorizing it under irreversible methods is wrong. Dr. Clive Wood, however, has warned: "Many experts believe that vasectomy should be regarded as an irreversible procedure. There are some doctors who have specialized in rejoining the cut ends of the vas, in response to requests from patients who have decided they would like to have their fertility restored, and some of these doctors have reported considerable success in restoring sperm to the semen in 50% of the cases or more. The return of fertility, however, cannot be guaranteed. And since this is so, patients who are likely to change their mind afterwards are not generally regarded as good candidates for the operation."[7]

Dr. al Buti states that the *'Ulama* unanimously agree it is not permissible to make use of any device that might permanently incapacitate a person, either man or woman, from procreation whether or not either or both spouses consent.[8] From the context it is not clear whether or not Dr. al Buti's statement refers to unquestionably irreversible methods of contraception for non-therapeutic reasons.

The Qur'an says:

Let those who find not the wherewithal for marriage keep

themselves chaste until Allah gives them the means out of His Grace (24:33).

Ibn Kathir, in his Commentary on the above verse, says that this is an order from Allah (SWT) for the one who is not in a position to marry to (keep one's chastity) by not indulging in what is forbidden, in accordance with the sayings of the Prophet (SAWS): "Whoever is not in a position (to marry) should fast for it is a means of curbing (one's passion)."[9] Curbing one's passion does not mean to destroy it completely, as Imam al Nawawi points out, for destroying it with the (intake) of camphor or any other similar thing is a type of castration, and castration is haram (prohibited).[10] On castration there are significant *Ahadith*.

1) Sa'd ibn Abi Waqqas said: "Allah's Messenger (SAWS) objected to 'Uthman ibn Maz'un living in celibacy. If he had given him permission (to do so) we (others) would have had ourselves castrated."[11]
2) 'Abd Allah bin Mas'ud reported, "We were on expedition with the Prophet (SAWS) and we had no women with us. We said, 'Should we not have ourselves castrated?' He (the Prophet) forbade us to do so."[12]

No doubt castration is unlike vasectomy, as Clive Wood points out: "Castration involves removing the testicles or testes, organs which produce not only sperms but also the male hormones that are essential to maintain a man's masculinity, including his sexual drive.... it (vasectomy) does not produce the state of weakness and indifference which is normally believed to accompany castration."[13]

The *'Ulama* apparently declared irreversible contraception *haram* (forbidden) using the analogy that castration was forbidden by the Prophet (SAWS). Tahir Mahmood disagrees with such an analogy. He states: "In coitus interruptus (which Islam permits) the man keeps his sperm away from the woman and for this he has to make a special effort in every act of coitus. Vasectomy is a surgical process through which the same effect is achieved on a permanent or long-term basis....Most certainly it is not forced impotency, because the sexual power of a man who undergoes sterilization remains absolutely unaffected. The Islamic ban on forced impotency can therefore have no application to vasectomy."[14]

It is true that vasectomy is unlike castration. But the similarity between the two is that castration renders one permanently incapable of engaging in sexual intercourse, and hence a castrated person cannot procreate his own species. In the same way a man who has undergone vasectomy cannot procreate. Vasectomy cannot be likened to coitus interruptus (*'azl*) because there exists in the latter the possibility of pregnancy occurring through involuntary pre-emission of semen, while vasectomy frustrates that possibility.

Again, Tahir Mahmood tries to justify tubal ligation, which he terms "tubectomy," by saying that he does not see any difference between the sealing of the womb by inserting an obstruction and producing the same effect by a surgical process. So he contends that if the former is valid under Islamic Law then logically there should be nothing illegal in the latter either. He alleges that the Shafi'i jurist Ibn Hajar referred to this device as "*ma yuqti al habla min aslihi*" (something that cuts the vein from its roots) and argues that Ibn Hajar permitted even the suspension of the oviducts.[15]

Several objections can be made to this interpretation. First, the above-quoted Arabic sentence, which appears in Ibn Hajar's work, *Fath al Bari*, should be transliterated as follows: "*ma yuqti' al habala min aslihi*" which means "that which prevents pregnancy from its very beginning." In our understanding this would refer to the woman taking measures like sealing of the womb to prevent pregnancy and certainly does not refer to the suspension of the oviducts or fallopian tubes. Second, Ibn Hajar does not give any verdict . He states merely that the later Shafi'i jurists forbid female use of contraceptives but he (Ibn Hajar) thinks that such prohibition conflicts with their absolute permission (with or without the wife's consent) of *'azl* (coitus interruptus). Thirdly, tubal ligation as a measure of sterilizing women was not possible when Ibn Hajar lived (1372-1449 A.C.). Norman E. Himes published an extensive survey in *Medical History of Contraception* and dealt with the various methods that were prescribed by the Muslim physicians, for example Ibn Sina (d. 1037), Isma'il al Jurjani (d. 1136), Ibn al Baytar (d. 1248), and Dawud al Antaki (d. 1599). He found that none of them spoke of female sterilization as a means of contraception.[17] It was only al Razi (d. 924) who pointed to possible male sterilization through "spoiling" the testicles with poison hemlock. But this technique was not mentioned by later physicians in their writings on contraceptive methods.[18]

The 'Ulama's stand against irreversible contraception is based on the ground that the Prophet (SAWS) forbade castration. The following arguments may be put forward in support of this claim:

First, both castration and irreversible contraceptive methods are contrary to the goals or objectives (*maqasid*) of the *Shari'ah* which uphold the institution of marriage as an essential means to pursue the first-order purpose of procreating the human species.

Secondly, both castration and irreversible contraceptive methods are tantamount to challenging the very nature or order of things as created by Allah (SWT). As pointed out by the Qur'an, attempting to change the natural order is submitting to the purpose of the devil, whom Allah (SWT) promised would deceive mankind by ordering persons "to deface the (fair) nature created by Allah" (4:119). Commenting on this verse, Muhammad Asad says, "The allusion to Satan's inducing man to 'corrupt' (lit., 'change') God's creation has a meaning to which sufficient attention is but seldom paid. Since this creation, and the manner in which it manifests itself, is an expression of God's planning will, any attempt at changing its intrinsic nature amounts to corruption."[19]

Nevertheless, if the woman's health or life would be threatened in any way by pregnancy, or if she develops cancer of the womb, then sterilizing her by resorting to tubal ligation or total hysterectomy would become an obligation. This obligation derives from the "rule of necessity" which brings to bear the higher priority of the first-order goal, right to life.

How should a Muslim doctor respond when asked to prescribe certain contraceptive means? Reversible contraception, as we have seen, is not prohibited (*haram*), i.e. inherently and absolutely forbidden, but is regarded as *makruh* (undesirable, improper). Hence it would be *makruh* also on the part of the Muslim doctor to prescribe such devices to his patients, unless the reasons against their use are more than outweighed by the requirments of health and life. In this case it would be his duty to prescribe such devices. Since it was pointed out earlier that the classical Muslim physicians did prescribe certain types of contraceptive devices, it would be instructive for the Muslim doctor today to know the reasons for which his predecessors prescribed such devices. Their understanding of the internal logic of the *Shari'ah* no doubt exceeded what we find today. For example, in discussing medical birth control measures, 'Ali ibn 'Abbas (d.994) states that "it is necessary sometimes to prescribe them to women with a small uterus, or who have a disease that in case of pregnancy might cause the woman's death in childbirth."[20] Ibn Sina (d. 1037) justified contraception on the following medical grounds: "The physician may be obliged to prevent pregnancy in a young woman for fear of her death in childbirth; or in a woman who suffers from a disease of the uterus; or in a woman whose bladder is weak. In the latter case the weight of the fetus may rupture the bladder, resulting in urinary incontinence lasting all her life."[21]

In summary, we have seen that the only type of contraceptive method in vogue during the time of the Prophet (SAWS) was *al 'azl* or coitus interruptus. Today, biomedical sciences have succeeded in perfecting new techniques that may be categorized as reversible and irreversible methods of contraception. Some of these modern methods are for male use, while others are for the female. We have pointed out that Ibn Taymiyyah did not condemn female use of contraceptives but cautioned women not to use them, while Ibn Nujaym sanctioned female use of contraceptives on the analogy that *'azl* was permissible as a male precautionary measure against pregnancy. Many scholars have advocated the use of modern reversible techniques. Though *makruh*, they are not prohibited (*haram*). In choosing any of these methods a woman should be careful that such a method will not be hazardous to her health in any way.

Concerning the irreversible methods the jurists have used the prohibition of castration as an analogy to reach a consensus that such irreversible methods of sterilizing men and women are not permissible. They contradict the objectives of Islamic law, which bestows high priority on the institution of marriage for the purpose of procreation. Irreversible sterilization also is an affront to the nature of things created by Allah (SWT).

CHAPTER VI
BIRTH CONTROL IN HISTORY

I. THE BIRTH CONTROL MOVEMENT

More then a millennium ago, al-Jahiz (d.868 A.C.) in his book, *The Animal Kingdom* (*Al-Hayawan*), distinguished man from other animals in man's ability to practice contraception.[1]

Coitus interruptus (withdrawal) may be the most ancient and natural form of birth control. We have seen that it was a practice prevalent in Arabia during the life of the Prophet of Islam (SAWS). He did not categorically forbid his followers from engaging in this practice nor did he encourage them in such a practice. Hence the unanimous opinion of all the schools of Islamic law is that this practice is *makruh* (undesirable) but not *haram* (forbidden).

There is a passage in the Bible which refers to the "sin of Onan" (Genesis 38:9). This passage tells us that Onan was destroyed because "he spilled his seed on the ground". Although this passage may not have been the basis for the earlier Christian thinking against contraception, nevertheless both Judaism and Christianity regarded the destruction of the semen as a wrongful act. Feldman explains that after the modern introduction of the pill, a change occured in the Jewish thinking on contraception, because the pill does nothing directly to the male sperm.[2]

The Christian stand on contraception evolved, in part, in the series of Lambeth Conferences. The 1920 Conference issued a warning against the use of all unnatural means to avoid conception. In 1930 and subsequently in 1958, however, it was agreed that on mutual consent the husband and wife could do what they felt best in deciding whether they should adopt contraceptive methods. This gave rise to the idea of responsible parenthood. The much stricter Roman Catholic stand on contraception was announced by Pope Pius XII on October 29, 1951, in his verbal public declaration that Christians may use only the rhythm method.[3]

The father of the birth control movement may be said to be Reverend Thomas R. Malthus, who was an Anglican clergyman and a famous English economist. In 1798, he published an essay "On Principles of Population as It Affects the Future Improvement of Society."[4] He did not recommend the use of contraceptives but, rather, advocated late marriage and self-restraint in matrimonial life in order to keep the population in check. The movement gained momentum when Francis Place of France stressed the necessity of making use of contraceptives in order to control the population. Subsequently, a revolutionary step was taken in that direction when Dr. Charles Knowlton published his book, *The Fruits of Philosophy*, in 1833 in America. In this work the use of contraceptives was explained from the medical point of view. But it was not until 1878 that the movement began to be taken seriously, when Mrs. Annie Besant published her best selling book, *Law of Population*.

From 1881 onwards birth control was practiced in Europe and America. The success of this movement may be ascribed to the Industrial Revolution in Europe. People who lived in the rural areas flocked into the urban areas in search of jobs in the factories. This caused the cities to be overpopulated. Housing became a problem. Taking advantage of the situation, rents were raised. It became difficult to manage a large family. Women were forced to leave their homes in search of work in order to bring revenue to the family. Thus, it was impractical for them to become pregnant often, because that would be neither in their interest nor in their employers'. So, they had to make use of contraceptive devices.[5]

The salient difference between the birth control movement in Europe and in the so called Third World Countries is the source of initiative. In Europe the people themselves resorted to contraceptive devices, whereas in the Third World governments intervened directly. They imposed family planning programs on a national scale. This was prompted by the high birth rates and the accelerating discrepancy between the high population growth and the low rate of economic growth. Among Muslim countries that were pioneers in implementing such programs are Pakistan, Turkey, Egypt, and Tunisia.[6] We shall analyse the implementation of the family program in Pakistan and the reactions to it.

II. Family Planning in Pakistan

When Pakistan attained its independence from Britain in 1947, there was speculation that the country might face the problem of overpopulation. Only after almost two decades, however, did the leaders of that country begin to take the problem seriously. Provision was made in the third five-year plan (1965-70) to educate and motivate experts in the establishment of family planning services throughout the country. As a result, a separate division of family planning (*Mahkamah-e-Khandani* Munsoobahbandi) was set up in the Ministry of Health, Labour, and Social Welfare to ensure that the newly adopted national policy be implemented. This plan allocated as much as 155 million rupees toward that end in the then undivided Pakistan.[7]

In order to justify the implementation of family planning, the Ministry of Health, Labour, and Social Welfare issued a declaration that the Qur'an does not raise any objections to the practice of family planning. Moreover, it added that the Prophet (SAWS) allowed his followers to practice birth control and that supporting evidence could be found in a number of *ahadith*. Furthermore, it emphasized that al Ghazali and Ibn Taymiyyah were in favor of birth control. Finally, it contended that the classical *'Ulama* gave their approval to more than one form of contraceptive methods.[8]

Although there is no categorical statement in the Qur'an condemning birth control, and the Prophet (SAWS) himself did not stop his followers from engaging in *'azl*, it was certainly untenable for the ministry to declare that the classical *'Ulama* gave a *carte blanche* to the practice of birth control. Athough it is not *haram* (forbidden), it is *makruh* (undesirable). Even though some of the classical *'Ulama*, like al Ghazali, allowed the practice of birth control for certain specific reasons, this prerogative was understood to be voluntary. The reasons for practicing it would naturally differ from individual to individual. What the government was calling for was affirmative action at the national level in implementing family planning throughout society. The *'Ulama* in Pakistan naturally denounced this policy as alien to Islam. Among those foremost in their condemnation of this policy were Sayyid Abu al 'Ala Mawdudi, of the Jama't-e-Islami, Mufti Muhammad Shafi', of the Dar al 'Uloom, Karachi, and Ihtisham al Haq Thanvi, also of Karachi. The *'Ulama* wasted no time in voicing their objections. They made use of the platforms in the mosques throughout the country as well as their pens in reaction against this national policy. Their arguments against family planning may be summarized as follows:

1) Family planning is akin to infanticide.
2) Family planning is unnatural or contrary to human nature (*ghayr fitri*).
3) Family planning is based on disbelief in the providence of Allah (SWT).
4) Family planning would be tantamount to ignoring the Prophet's wish that Muslims should increase in number.
5) Family planning will lead to disastrous social consequences.
6) Family planning is a sort of a conspiracy of the Western imperialists against the developing nations.

On the other hand, there were some scholars like Dr. Fazlur Rahman, the then Director of the Islamic Research Institute, Islamabad, Khalifa Abdul Hakim, Akhtar Hameed Khan, and Muhammad Shahidullah who supported the family planning programs. They felt it their duty to refute the objections put forth by the *'Ulama* against family planning. For example, Khalifa Abdul Hakim argued that birth control could not be recognized as infanticide for if this were true then parents by the millions would have had to mourn their loss of children after every interrupted sexual intercourse.[9] Muhammad Shahidullah argued that practicing birth control in no way means that one does not have faith in the providence of Allah (SWT). He remarked that Islam and commonsense would not approve of married people with insufficent means continuing to beget children who could neither be fed nor given proper education.[10] In refuting the *'Ulama's* fourth objection, Dr. Fazlur Rahman pointed out that on the Day of Judgement the Prophet (SAWS) would not be proud of a numerically large ummah composed of "semi-starved weaklings, diseased persons, and ignorant men and women."[11]

The *'Ulama's* second and the last two objections, however, may be justified. We must try to understand, first,, that when the *'Ulama* described family planning as unnatural, they were fully aware that if family planning were to be enacted as a national policy then it would be difficult to stop usage of irreversible methods. We saw, earlier on, that Islamic jurisprudence regards such methods as *haram* (forbidden), based on the analogy that the Prophet (SAWS) forbade his followers to castrate themselves. Second, the *'Ulama* were concerned that making birth control devices freely available could lead to the rise of sexual perversion or promiscuity within the society. And it is true that organizations like the International Monetary Fund (IMF) practically refuse to allocate loans to Third World Countries unless and until they promise to implement family planning schemes.

A question that remains to be answered is whether any of the principles of Islamic jurisprudence could be used to justify Pakistan's stand on the implementation of family planning on a national scale? Mawdudi may be correct in pointing out that "as regards Pakistan, it could be said without any fear that the economic problems that confront us are more a product of our own mistakes and shortsighted policies and less of the niggardliness of nature."[12] But, knowing the cause of the problem does not help in solving the problem. There must be a determination to do something to rectify the situation once the problem is identified. Again, waiting for good times when the situation would be rectified and at the same time allowing the population to grow without attempting to put a check on it would be tantamount to lack of prudence. Thus it is that Dr.Fazlur Rahman holds the view that it may be justified to apply the juristic principle of *al masalih al mursalah* (general welfare) to implement family planning as a national policy in the event that the country faces genuine overpopulation problems. He states, "This juristic principle makes provision to give primacy to problems concerning the wealth and welfare of the community."13 On this issue, the author would opt to take the stand of the traditional *'Ulama*, who strongly oppose the implementation of family planning on a national scale. When contraceptive devices are made freely available to the people there is absolutely no doubt that it would eventually lead to sexual permissiveness. Since more harm would result thereby, the author fails to see the justification for family planning on a national scale on the basis of the juristic principle of *al masalih al mursalah*. What would apparently seem to be in the interest of the general welfare of the *ummah* would turn out to be against its interest. Thus, another juristic principle, namely "that which leads to prohibited things is prohibited" will take precedence over the principle of *al masalih al mursalah*.

PART THREE:

BIOTECHNICAL PARENTING

CHAPTER VII
THE PROBLEM OF INFERTILITY

Infertility can be defined as the failure to produce a viable pregnancy within a year of regular sexual intercourse without the use of contraceptives.[1] This problem is not new. In the annals of history it has been experienced by different communities, and people have tried to overcome it in various ways. This chapter concerns the means the Muslims used to cope with the problem throughout the ages before the recent breakthroughs in the field of biomedical science.

I. THE QUR'AN AND INFERTILITY

Procreation of the human species is part of the divine plan and this is brought out clearly in the following verse of the Qur'an: "O mankind! Reverence your Guardian-Lord, Who created you from a single Person, created of like nature his mate, and from them twain scattered (like seeds) countless men and women" (4:1). Muslims look forward to having children and they are well aware of the *hadith* of their Prophet (SAWS): "Marry women who will love you and give birth to many children for I shall take pride in the great number of my *ummah* (nation)."[2]

But, at the same time, they firmly believe that nothing happens except as willed by Allah (SWT). Referring to the bestowing of children and infertility or barrenness, the Qur'an states:

> To Allah belongs the dominion of the heavens and the earth. He creates what He wills (and plans). He bestows (children) male or female according to His will (and plan). Or He bestows both males and females, and He leaves barren whom He wills: for He is full of Knowledge and Power (42:49-50).

Commenting on this verse, Ibn Kathir says that Allah (SWT) informs us that it is He Who is the Creator of the heavens and the earth, and that He alone decides what is to take place in them. He gives to whom He pleases and holds back his bounties from whom He pleases. He creates whatever He wishes. He may bestow (to a couple) only female children and to another males only, while to yet another He may bless them with both males and females and may even leave some of the people barren.[3]

The Qur'an does make reference to at least two Prophets, namely Zakariyya and Ibrahim (AS), whose wives could not bear children but eventually did in their old age. The Qur'an records the words uttered by Zakariyya and the wife of Ibrahim, on being given the glad tidings that they would be blessed with offspring, in the following manner:

> He [Zakariyya] said, "O my Lord! How shall I have a son, seeing that I am very old, and my wife is barren?" "Thus," was the answer, "does Allah accomplish what He will" (3:40); She [Sarah, wife of Ibrahim] said, "Alas for me! Shall I bear a child, seeing I am an old woman, and my husband here is an old man? That would indeed be a wonderful thing!" (11:72).

Thus, from the references made to infertility or barrenness in the Qur'an, it is clear that some people may not be able to bear children but nevertheless can if it is the will of Allah (SWT).

II. COPING WITH INFERTILITY

Muslims who are not blessed with offspring are, generally speaking, hopeful that they would one day be blessed with children in the same way as Prophets Ibrahim and Zakariyya (AS). Hence their very first move is to beseech Allah (SWT) to cure them of their barrenness. But, it has to be noted that though the invoking of Allah may be their first response, nevertheless, there are other ways and means by which the Muslims in different parts of the globe have responded to the problem. Some of them resorted to polygamy, others by seeking help through amulets or *ta'widh*, and yet others chose to take foster children. We shall now deal with these three methods separately.

Unrestricted polygamy (plurality of wives) was the norm in pre-Islamic Arabia, and with the advent of Islam the maximum number of wives that one could have at one time was limited to four.[4] The relevant Qur'anic passage dealing with this subject reads as follows:

> And if you fear that you shall not be able to deal justly with the orphans, marry of the women who seem good to you, two or three, or four; but if you fear that (in case of having more wives than one) you shall not be able to deal justly (with them) then (marry) only one (free woman) or (a captive) that your right hands possess. That will be more suitable to prevent you from doing injustice (4:3).

From the above passage, it is evident that polygamy is not a compulsory institution, but rather is permissible with certain conditions and under certain circumstances. Islam allows polygamy, for example, as a means to curb promiscuity in societies where women out-number men. Or, it may, as Dr. Hammudah 'Abd al 'Ati puts it, "permit a man, whose wife is not capable of having children for some reason or other, to remarry in order to satisfy his natural needs and at the same time maintain his childless wife, who probably needs him now more than at any other time."[5] It is appropriate, however, to point out that polygamy is not a common practice among the Muslims in general.

Muslims in the Indo-Pak subcontinent try to resolve the problem of infertility by visiting certain "spiritual masters," who are commonly referred to as *pirs*, in order that they pray for them to be cured of their barrenness. Normally, such a *pir* would give the husband concerned an amulet and ask that it be tied around the waist of his wife.[6] It cannot be denied that in some cases an infertile woman wearing such an amulet somehow or other becomes pregnant. Such an event is then interpreted by the people who have "faith" in such practices as due to the effective power of the mulet.

Adoption or foster-parenting is perhaps the best option. In South Africa, a number of people have been foster-parented by childless aunts and uncles, either maternal or paternal. It seems that in South Africa the Muslims try to resolve their problem of not being able to have offspring by foster-parenting the children of either their brothers or sisters. The *Shari'ah* prohibits Muslims from legally adopting children of other parents. The Qur'an is explicit on this issue:

> Allah has not made for any man two hearts in his (one) body: Nor has He made your wives whom you divorce by *zihar* your mothers: Nor has He made your adopted sons your sons. Such is (only) your (manner of) speech by your mouths. But, Allah tells you the Truth and He shows the (Right) way (33:4).
>
> Call them by (the names of) their fathers: that is more just in the sight of Allah. But if you know not their father's (names, call them) your brothers in faith, or your *Mauwlas* (fostered ones). But, there is no blame if you make a mistake therein: (what counts is) the intention of your hearts: and Allah is Oft-Returning, Most Merciful (33:5).

Ibn Kathir, explains that these verses were revealed in regard to Zayd bin Harithah (RA) whom the Prophet (SAWS) adopted as his own son before the prophethood was conferred upon him. He was therefore called Zayd bin Muhammad, and Allah (SWT) wished that this affixation and relationship (i.e., bin Muhammad which means son of Muhammad) be discontinued. Moreover, adopting someone and claiming him as your own in no way makes him truly your child for he is the generation of another man and it is not possible for him to have two fathers in the same way as it is impossible for a man to possess two hearts.[7]

Dr. Hammudah 'Abd al 'Ati tries to explain the wisdom in forbidding Muslims from adopting children in the legal sense by stating that "adoption is one of the major reasons that encourage many people to indulge in irresponsible activities and intimacies. It is being commercialized nowadays. There are some people who put up their children for 'sale' or trade as the news media show. That is not in the African or Asian jungles; it is right here in Canada and America. Because of all that, Islam does not accept the institution or tolerate its practice among Muslims."[8] Dr. 'Abd al 'Ati fails to bring out the wisdom in the Qur'anic prohibition of legal adoption. He seems to have missed the point altogether. For certainly the Qur'anic injunction in this regard could not have been motivated by the fact that the institution could possibly be abused. It must be pointed out that though the Qur'an condemns legal adoption, it, on the other hand, strongly supports the fostering of orphans and exhorts Muslims to uphold this practice. When fostering a child of someone else, its family name will remain the same, unlike in adoption which makes it lose its family name. The reason for having the child retain its family name is to prevent it getting married accidentally to its own blood sister or brother. Moreover, the Qur'an prevents inbreeding, and details in this regard are found in surah 4, entitled al Nisa', verses 23-24.

We have seen that infertility is the failure to produce offspring. The Qur'an points out that it is Allah (SWT) Who bestows progeny upon some people. Others He chooses to leave barren. Muslims have reacted positively in trying to resolve the problem. But the practicality of the steps they took is subject to criticism. For example, polygamy may resolve the problem of a man whose wife cannot bear children by permitting him to marry another woman in order to beget children by her. But, if the defect lies in the man, polygamy will not solve his problem, nor would it satisfy his barren wife's innate craving to be a mother. Biologically speaking, because of her physiological nature, it is the woman who has a greater urge to have her own children. Should not something be done therefore to assist her in solving her infertility problem?

Again, resorting to the *pirs* for assistance through the means of amulets in no way guarantees solving the problem of infertility. Moreover, fostering a child, namely an orphan, may be a meritorious act and may give the couple involved the pleasure of rearing a child and looking after his or her welfare. But that child can never be called their own and can in no way take the name of the foster father; nor can he or she be the legal heir of the foster parents. Of the three solutions enumerated above, foster parenting is the most practical solution for the barren couple in the sense that both of them can equally share in the joy of rearing a child; though not their own, the foster-child may still be brought up as if he or she were their own offspring.

Our purpose in showing how Muslims tried to solve the problem of infertility is to show that they at least coped with the situation in a positive manner, rather than giving up all hope and succumbing to depression.

CHAPTER VIII
BIOMEDICAL SCIENCE AND INFERTILITY

It is appropriate to understand the process by which pregnancy normally occurs before dealing with the biomedical analysis of the problem of infertility and the biotechnical possibilities of helping people become parents.

At the time of intercourse, sperm is ejaculated by the man into the upper part of the vagina of the woman. These sperm swim through the cervix (the mouth of the womb), through the cavity within the body of the uterus (womb), and through the fallopian tubes.

In the female, ovulation takes place every month. During ovulation one or more ova (eggs) are pushed out of the ovary where it has been growing. Finger-like projections at the end of the fallopian tube pick up this expelled ovum (or ova) and pass it into the tube.

If the timing is correct, then the sperm and ovum will come into contact with each other in the tube and the egg will be fertilized. The fertilized egg then divides into a number of cells. This ball of cells then begins its movement down the tube. After about three days, it reaches the body of the uterus and is implanted into its wall and begins to grow and develop into a baby.[1]

I. CAUSES OF INFERTILITY

Biomedical science has succeeded in pointing out that infertility may be caused by certain "defects" either in the wife or husband.

Male infertility may be due to the abnormality of the sperm in the sense that there is a low sperm count and poor sperm movement. This may result from excessive heat, such as frequent use of hot tubs, or the wearing of tight-fitting jockey shorts, or contracting mumps after puberty, which may cause permanent damage to the testes. Or, infertility may result from certain anatomic abnormalities such as varicocele, i.e., an abnormality of the veins surrounding the testes, and undescended testicles, a birth-defect that leads to infertility if untreated. Sometimes corrective surgery may cause irreversible damage. Likewise, the ducts that carry the sperm from the testes to the penis may be blocked. Or infertility may result from reverse ejaculation whereby the male ejaculates in the reverse direction so that the semen enters the bladder instead of going out through the tip of the penis. This may occur as a result of severe diabetes, neurological disease, or prostatic surgery.[2]

Female infertility may result from the absence of or a blockage of the fallopian tubes. Closure of the tubes may occur especially as a result of sexually transmitted diseases or occasionally from an infection originating from within the abdomen – for example, from a ruptured appendix. Or the tubes may also be damaged by handling during pelvic surgery. Another problem may be associated with the failure to ovulate (anovulation), so that no egg emerges from the ovary, in which case there may be a problem in the uterus, vagina, ovary, or pituary gland. Or female infertility may result from an allergy to the proteins contained in the semen. Sometimes, the female may be born without a uterus and fertility in such a case is virtually impossible.[3]

II. CURES

In order to help a couple overcome infertility and become parents, biomedical science has devised certain ways and means. Paul D. Simmons has elaborated these possibilities, as summarized below.[4]

Artificial insemination (AI) involves using the husband's (AIH) or a donor's (AID) sperm to impregnate a woman. A physician introduces sperm into the woman's uterus, where, it is hoped, it will fertilize the awaiting ovum. The sperm may be fresh or supplied from a sperm bank, where semen is frozen and stored.

In vitro fertilization (IVF) involves extracting a ripened ovum from a woman's ovary, fertilizing it in a petri dish in the laboratory, and returning the embryo to the woman's uterus, where it is hoped the ovum will attach to the wall of the uterus and develop to a normal birth.

Egg transfer involves transfering an egg from a donor woman to an infertile woman's uterus. The egg may be fertilized by the recipient's husband.

Artificial embryonation (AE) requires flushing an embryo from a woman who has been inseminated artificially by a donor's sperm, then implanting the embryo in the womb of the donor's wife.

Embryo adoption (EA), or prenatal adoption, involves both donor sperm and donor egg, but they would be transferred to the womb of the recipient and she would bring the fetus to birth.

Ectogenesis is the nurture of a fetus from fertilization to viability in an artificial placenta or glass womb.

Cloning, or nuclear transplant, consists of removing the nucleus of an egg and replacing this with the nucleus of a donated unfertilized egg or the nucleus of a body cell. The renucleated cell is then implanted and brought to term in the womb. The child has only the genetic material of the donor of the nucleus. Since only a male or female seed is used, this is a process without conception. It is artificial virgin birth - a child with the same DNA as the (one) parent. This has not as yet been carried out.

Surrogate parenting involves a woman bearing a child for another woman, one who is presumably infertile. The surrogate mother is artificially impregnated with the contracting husband's sperm.

The contribution of biomedical science in determining the salient factors involved in infertility can hardly be underestimated. The biomedical possibilities, mentioned above, bring hope to the childless couples, but such techniques, in efforts to solve the problem of infertility, raise a number of ethical and legal questions or issues and thus cannot be given blanket approval.

In the next chapter, an attempt is made to bring out the ethical issues involved and to analyze the techniques within the Islamic framework.

CHAPTER IX

ANALYSIS OF THE BIOTECHNICAL METHODS

When Muslims object to specific biotechnical methods, this does not mean that Islam is against technological advancement or progress. Nor, does it imply, as Sania Hamady contends, that Muslims are fatalists:

> The teaching that predominates in the Koran is determinism. All things were created by Allah by degrees and all things in the lives of men and other creatures are set down beforehand in books, with the prevailing view that the events of a person's life are determined from the very beginning. Not even in everyday life can man do anything to hasten or otherwise influence what is going to happen to him. Predestination makes him skeptical with regard to control over his own future actions or events, and creates an improvident outlook and excuses to relegate responsibility to external sources.[1]

The Qur'an does speak of predestination in regard to the creation of the various things in the world, but that means that the natural properties ingrained in these things have already been predetermined. Also in the case of man's creation, the way he is physically constituted has already been predetermined. The Qur'an does not maintain that man is predetermined in his actions.

The Qur'an speaks of man as being neither completely determined nor completely free, i.e., he has limited choice. Moreover, man does not possess knowledge of the future, and that is why sometimes his actions lead to success and at other times to failure. The knowledge of Allah (SWT) does not relate in any way to predetermination or predestination as such. Let us take as an example a man lighting a candle in front of a child and leaving the candle on the table. He knows that the child would be tempted to touch the flame, but his knowing that does not determine the action of the child.

Medical intervention, is thoroughly Islamic. The well-known saying of the Prophet (SAWS), " for every disease there is a cure",[2] led the Muslims eventually to probe into the science of medicine and to make great contributions in this field.[3] If Muslims had been skeptical, as Sania Hamady claims, then their actions and contributions would be inexplicable. It would have been more appropriate for them to resign themselves to the mercy of Allah (SWT) when inflicted with a disease rather than attempt to seek medical attention. But history bears witness to the fact that this was not the attitude of the Muslims. The Prophet (SAWS), who received the revelation of the Qur'an, in reality exhorted his companions to seek medical attention whenever they fell ill.

The first possible objection to biotechnical solutions for the problem of infertility concerns their justification. Don't they tamper with the *Sunan* (Ways) of Allah? Might not such technology lead to a dystopia like the one Aldous Huxley depicts in his novel *Brave New World*?[4] It is true that such technology may be abused. But we should look at the positive aspect of such technology. A knife can prove disastrous if misused, but has numerous benefits if used correctly.

Such technology to resolve infertility cannot be condemned outright as being against the *Sunan* of Allah (SWT) because infertility should be viewed as a "defect" or "disease." And the saying of the Prophet (SAWS) that "for every disease there is a cure" gives Muslims the impetus to try to do something about it. For example, the cause of infertility in the man or woman concerned may be rectified through corrective surgery, as in the case where the ducts that carry the sperm from the testes to the penis, or the fallopian tubes in the case of the woman, may be blocked. No doubt trying to resolve the problem of infertility by technological means does not guarantee its solution but it is a positive attempt in that direction.

Methods other than corrective surgery, however, involve certain ethical or legal issues. Let us now attempt to evaluate these techniques separately by applying the ethical principles of Islamic law.

I. ARTIFICIAL INSEMINATION (AI) AND MASTURBATION

Artificial insemination (AI) is the procedure whereby a semen specimen is placed in a syringe attached to a narrow tube or catheter and subsequently that catheter is inserted with great care into the cervical canal and the semen is slowly injected into the uterus. The woman accepting the sperm in this fashion has to be in a position whereby her hips are raised and remain in that position for fifteen or twenty minutes so as to increase the chances of the sperm fertilizing the ovum.[5]

The question now is how the sperm in the above mentioned procedure is to be obtained? Doctors Robert H. Glass, M.D., and Ronald J. Ericsson, Ph.D., state : "Attempts to collect the semen by withdrawing during intercourse are usually unsuccessful because the first few drops, which contain the greatest concentration of sperm, frequently are lost thus making the sperm count falsely low. Collection into a condom also does not work because condoms contain certain spermicidal agents, and the laboratory will find only dead sperm. For those males who cannot, or will not, masturbate to collect a specimen, there is a special sheath that does not contain a spermicide, and it can be used for collection of the specimen during intercourse."[6]

From the above it is evident that the only two ways in which sperm may be obtained is either by masturbation or the inserting of the penis inside a special sheath, which does not contain a spermicide, prior to intercourse. In the event that this special sheath is not easily available, the only way to collect the semen would be through masturbation. Here is where the problem arises. A spokesman for the Islamic Medical Association of South Africa on being questioned by the *Daily News Reporter*, Durban, about the Islamic view on test-tube babies, said:

> But obtaining the male sperm would involve masturbation and this went against Islamic law.[7]

All four of the major schools of Islamic law view masturbation as a sin but prescribe no specific punishment or even reprimand for the one who engages in it.

The basis for it being regarded as a prohibited act under Islamic law is the Qur'anic verse which states:

> (The Believers) are those who abstain from sex, except with those joined to them in the marriage bond, or those whom their right hands possess - for (in their case) they are free from blame (23:5-6).

To use the sexual organ other than in the way specified in the above verse would be tantamount to disobeying the explicit command of Allah (SWT). This would render one a transgressor as indicated in the subsequent verse:

> But those who desire to exceed those limits are transgressors (23:7).

The Maliki School infers from the words of the Prophet (SAWS) that masturbation is prohibited (*haram*):

> He who is able to marry should marry for it keeps the gaze low and guards one's chastity; but he who cannot (marry) should resort to fasting (occasionally), for it will help curb one's sexual passion.[8]

Hence, the jurists belonging to this school say that if masturbation were permitted under the *Shari'ah*, the Messenger of Allah (SWT) would have pointed it out, since it is an easier act (to engage in) than fasting. So, the fact that it was not pointed out signifies that it is a forbidden act.[9]

Presenting the opinion of the Shafi'i jurists on the issue, B.F. Musallam writes : "Still others, such as the strict Shafi'i jurist Nawawi, whose opinion is typical of the Shafi'i jurists as a whole, said that masturbation was absolutely forbidden (*haram*). But, then we find that he, as well as the other Shafi'is, permitted masturbation when it was performed by the hand of a man's wife or concubine, for he has a right to the enjoyment of her hand as he has to the rest of her body."[10]

'Abd al Rahman al Juzayri states: "The author of *Subul al Salam* says some of the Hanbali and Hanafi jurists are of the opinion that masturbation may be permissible in the event that one fears (that his not engaging in it) would lead to his committing adultery or fornication. But, he cautions that such a view is weak and is not to be relied upon."[11]

The consensus from the above is that masturbation is regarded as a forbidden (*haram*) act and is to be avoided. But the question before us now is whether it would be forbidden under Islamic law to masturbate in order to obtain the semen so as to have one's wife impregnated with it through artificial insemination. Support of permitting it should be argued on the basis that engaging in the act is not to derive pleasure but, rather, to obtain the semen for the specific purpose of trying to solve the problem of infertility. Permission would come from the purpose-oriented concept of the higher goals contained in the juristic principle that "necessity renders the forbidden permissible,"[12] as indicated in the Qur'anic verse:

> But whoso is compelled (thereto) by necessity, without wilful disobedience, not transgressing due limits, thy Lord is Forgiving, Most Merciful" (6:145).

II. SPERM DONORS

In some cases the husband may be unable to produce any sperm at all (a condition called azospermia). Or he may be suffering from a neurological condition that makes it impossible for him to ejaculate. Or he may be suffering from a certain disease like diabetes, for instance, which renders him impotent. Or he may be the carrier of a dominant gene for a genetic disorder (Huntington's Chorea, for example).[13] If any such condition prevails, then it is still possible to have one's wife inseminated with the sperm of a sperm donor. This accounts for the existence of sperm banks in certain advanced technological countries.

Pregnancy takes place when the sperm fertilizes the ovum, so the fetus or child that results out of the union can only be said to be the child of the biological parents. Now, the Qur'an recognizes the vital role that the sperm plays in human reproduction and states:

> Now let man but think from what he is created! He is created from a drop emitted (i.e. sperm) - proceeding from between the backbone and ribs (86:5-7).

But the Qur'an warns that this "seed" or sperm should not be misused, in the sense that its emission should occur only in the event of having sex with one's wife. This can be deduced from the verse wherein it describes as one of the qualities of believers that they have sex only with those who are joined to them in the marriage bond (23:5-6).

The question before us is whether Islamic law justifies the use of the sperm of someone other than that of the husband to be used in the process of artificially inseminating the woman? In this regard a former head of the Azhar University, Shaykh Mahmud Shaltut, issued the following religious decree (*fatwa*) condemning it and equating it to an adulterous act:

> Artificial insemination with the sperm of a foreign person, is, under the *Shari'ah*, a grievous crime and a great sin and is tantamount to adultery, for their essence is the same and their result is also the same. For, it is the insertion of the sperm of a foreign person intentionally into a tilth which has not been legally tied to him through the bond of marriage.... The legal verdict for artificial insemination in that way is the same as that of adultery which has been condemned and prohibited by the Divine Shari'ah.[14]

Dr. Yusuf al Qaradawi, addressing himself to the question of donor artificial insemination states:

> Islam safeguards lineage by prohibiting *zina* (adultery and fornication) and legal adoption, thus keeping the family line unambiguously defined without any foreign element entering into it. It likewise prohibits what is known as artificial insemination if the donor of the sperm is other than the husband.[15]

So, from what has been said above, sperm banks would be condemned by Islamic law in view of the fact that using any sperm other than that of the husband to impregnate one's wife is considered an illegitimate act. Moreover even if a husband has his sperm stored in a sperm bank, with the intention that if he dies his sperm can be used to impregnate his wife, this is illegal under Islamic law, because death renders the marriage union void, in the sense that a woman can marry someone else after a certain specified period - the *'iddat* (i.e., after four months and ten days).[16] So for the wife to be impregnated after her husband's death with his sperm would also be termed an illegitimate act.

Islam stands not alone in its condemnation of artificial insemination by a third party donor's sperm. Papal teaching rejects such artificial insemination within marriage. Pope Pius XII issued the following statement:

> Artificial fecundation within marriage, but produced by the active element of a third party is equally immoral and as such deserves unqualified condemnation.... The parents alone have a reciprocal right over each other's body to engender a new life, and this right is exclusive, perpetual, and inalienable. And this is as it should be, in consideration of the child. Nature imposes upon the ones who give life to a little being, in virtue of this bond between them, the task of conservation and education. But between the legitimate husband and that child, which, with his consent, is the fruit of the active element of a third party, there exists no bond of origin, no moral and juridical bond of conjugal procreation.[17]

In December 1945, the Archbishop of Canterbury appointed a commission to study the implication of artificial insemination. The report held that donor artificial insemination is intrinsically a breach of marriage, that it is adulterous and injurious to the child conceived and therefore "wrong in principle and contrary to Christian standards."[18]

A prominent Jewish view is expressed by Dr.Immanuel Jakobovits who says that a growing number of modern responses on the subject of A.I.D. unanimously and utterly condemn it.[19]

Impregnation of one's wife with the sperm of a sperm donor does not make the child one's own, and is looked upon as illegitimate even in man-made laws. In the United States some courts have viewed donor artificial insemination as adultery, and grounds for divorce. Moreover, in a few cases children by donor insemination have been declared illegitimate by the courts.[20]

In South Africa, the *Daily News* of Durban reported the following on the issue of donor artificial insemination:

> Children born when their mothers are artificially inseminated with the sperm of men not their husbands are strictly illegitimate, according to South African law.[21]

III. IN VITRO FERTILIZATION (IVF)

In vitro is a Latin phrase which means "in glass." In embryology it is used in contrast with "*in utero*" or "in the uterus." In normal circumstances, human fertilization takes place *in utero* (strictly speaking, in the fallopian tubes) when a sperm cell unites with an ovum. So, *in vitro* fertilization (IVF) is fertilization that is artificially performed outside the woman's body "in a test-tube."[22]

In vitro fertilization is a process that helps a woman overcome her infertility in cases where the woman's fallopian tubes may be absent, abnormal, or damaged.

There are four basic steps involved in the process of *in vitro* fertilization. First, the woman concerned is given a reproductive hormone in order to cause ova to ripen. A few hours before ovulation can be expected to occur, a small incision is made in the abdomen just below the navel. A laparoscope (an instrument with a built-in lens and light source) is inserted through the incision, and the ovaries are examined directly. When mature eggs are found that are about to break free from the thin walls of the ovarian follicle, the walls are punctured and the contents are removed by a vacuum respirator. Several eggs may be removed. Second, the eggs are transferred to a nutrient solution biochemically similar to that found in the fallopian tubes. Sperm is then added to the solution. As soon as a single sperm cell penetrates the ovum, the ovum is fertilized. Third, the fertilized egg is transferred to a nutrient solution where, after about a day, it begins to undergo cell division. When the ovum reaches the eight-cell stage, it is ready to be returned to the uterus. The woman concerned is then given injections of hormones so as to prepare her uterus to receive the fertilized egg. Fourth, the small ball of cells is placed in the uterus through the cervix (the opening that leads to the vagina) by means of a hollow plastic tube called a cannula. The fertilized egg continues to divide, and somewhere between the thirty-two and sixty-four cell stage, it attaches itself to the uterine wall. If the attachment is successful then from that time onwards development takes place as though fertilization had occurred in the normal fashion.[23]

The advantages of IVF may be enumerated as follows: 1) it meets the childbearing desire of the woman; 2) the child bears the genetic features of both married partners; and 3) there are no risks of strain between the married partners because of the contribution of another woman who might be perceived as a competitor.[24] Paul Ramsey, however, strongly opposes IVF and is of the opinion that it should not be carried out due to the great risk of genetic deformity.[25] Looking at it from the Islamic standpoint, it is true that IVF may help a woman beget offspring and thereby "cure" her of her infertility. But there are two issues involved in this procedure that make its legality questionable. First, only a single fertilized ovum is selected for implantation while all the other fertilized ova are simply discarded. Second, it may happen that while monitoring the development of the fertilized ovum after implantation has taken place, certain abnormalities may be detected that could tempt one to terminate the pregnancy. Discarding the fertilized ova and terminating the pregnancy on the grounds of abnormality would be questionable under Islamic law. Imam al Ghazali in his *Ihya Ulum al Din* stated a millenium ago:

> (Human) existence has stages. The first stages of existence are the settling of the semen in the womb and its mixing with the secretions of the woman. It is then ready to receive life. Disturbing it is a crime. When it develops further and becomes a lump, aborting it is a greater crime.[26]

Thus, it seems that the only way IVF could be acceptable under Islamic law as a means to overcome infertility is if the fertilization process outside the uterus is restricted to a single ovum. That would solve the problem of discarding other fertilized ova. But it may be argued that in normal circumstances, if more than one ovum are fertilized, nature takes care of that by expelling the other fertilized ova. Thus, would it not be equally justified to discard other fertilized ova and use only one of them for implantation?

IV. EGG TRANSFER, ARTIFICIAL EMBRYONATION, AND EMBRYO ADOPTION

Egg transfer involves the transfer of an egg of another woman into the uterus of one's wife, while artificial embryonation and embryo adoption involve the transfer of an already fertilized egg from another woman and placing it in the uterus of one's wife. If attachment to the uterine wall is successful, then development of the embryo would take place in the normal fashion.

These techniques are chosen if one's wife is not able to ovulate. Or perhaps she has no fallopian tubes at all, or there may be something abnormal causing blockage of the fallopian tubes or her tubes may be damaged. Clearly these three techniques can positively assist an infertile woman to bear and give birth to a child. The problem is that in the case of egg transfer the woman will bear a child with half of the genetic identity of her husband and none of her own. While in the case of artificial embryonation or embryo adoption (EA) the child would have the genetic complements neither of her husband nor of herself.

The Qur'an teaches that in the creation of mankind the roles of the males and females in the process are recognized. For example, it states:

> O mankind! We created you from a single (pair) of a male and a female (49:13).

And it emphasizes, the union should be legitimized through the marriage bond (23:5-6).

Thus, using the ovum or egg or an embryo of another woman even though it is transferred into the uterus of one's own wife, would be questionable under Islamic Law. And the above mentioned religious decree (*fatwa*) of Shaykh Shaltut against artificial insemination with the sperm of a donor, could apply equally, on the basis of analogy, against the adoption of such techniques to correct infertility.

V. ECTOGENESIS AND CLONING

This technique involves the nurture of a fetus from fertilization to viability in an artificial placenta or glass womb. If the sperm and ovum used in this process come from a legally married couple it appears that ectogenesis would not be illegal under Islamic law, especially if undertaking such a step is motivated by the simple reason that one's wife was born without a uterus.

As James B. Nelson points out, however, such a technology is still being developed. He mentions that the Italian embryologist Daniele Petrucci, who used this technology to sustain the life of an embryo for 29 days, destroyed it, for it was grossly deformed.[27]

Bernard Haering is critical of the prospect of childbearing by ectogenesis on still other grounds than the danger of deformity. In his opinion, this technique is a "loveless way" of producing a child. He even fears that such a person would suffer great damage psychologically and might not be in a position to reciprocate love.[28] Paul D. Simmons points out that such technology could even lead "to the suggestions that human embryos might be nurtured in the uterus of cows so as to relieve women of the maternal burden. Non-human environments ought not be used for human subjects. The development during gestation is important in caring for the humanity of the fetus."[29] The experimental results of the Italian embryologist, who had to kill the human form he brought about by ectogenesis, might make its legality in Islam at best questionable.

It seems that cloning would not fall under the category of trying to resolve the problem of infertility, because it is motivated rather for the satisfaction of one's own personal ego - to have a clone of oneself. Producing children in this manner would threaten the very institution of marriage, and therefore clearly would be an illegal venture under Islamic law.

VI. SURROGATE PARENTING

Surrogate parenting involves a woman bearing the child of another woman who is not in a position to bear children as a result of blocked fallopian tubes or lack of a uterus. To be a surrogate mother is, so to say, "leasing her womb"; for the child that one gives birth to does not "legally" become one's own but is the child of the couple who pays the surrogate mother for that particular purpose. In some of the states in America it is a legal venture. But in England it has not as yet been legalized.[30] This procedure no doubt allows an infertile couple to have a child who would have the genetic complement of the husband, if the husband's sperm is used to fertilize the ovum of the surrogate woman. But, the problem arises in fertilizing the ovum of another woman by the sperm of a man not her husband. Is this to be regarded as an adulterous union? Clearly it would be illegal under Islamic law.

The sperm and ovum of the married couple may also be fertilized *in vitro* and placed in the womb of a surrogate mother, who would be paid for giving birth to their child. The child would bear the full genetic complement of the contracting couple. It is relevant here that when Muslims have their children breast-fed by a foster mother, the childern would be like the child of the wet-nurse.

This means that if the wet-nurse has her own biological children, the childern she breast-fed would not legally be permitted to marry any of her own biological children.[31] But, it is to be emphasized that this prerogative of surrogate breast feeding can in no way serve as justification for the surrogate mother to carry to term the fertilized egg of the married couple. No parallel can be drawn between the wet-nurse and the surrogate mother. The wet-nurse provides the basic essential nourishment to the already born child, while the surrogate mother carries the "unformed" child to term and literally gives birth to it! This poses two immediate problems:

A. The Legality of the Contract

The contract which the surrogate mother and the married couple enters into can in no way be justified legally under the *Shari'ah* (Islamic Law). It would be considered a *baṭil* (invalid) contract. This stand may be clarified by pointing out that a sale contract would be legal only if it involves such transactions as are permissible under the *Shari'ah* . For example, no transaction involving the sale of or purchase of alcohol (intoxicating drinks) would be legally valid.[32] In the same manner, the contract between the married and the surrogate mother is invalid in the sense that 1) it is a contract stipulating the "sale" of a free person; and 2) it involves an element of adulterous implantation (the fertilized egg being implanted not in the wife but in the womb of the surrogate mother).

B. The Question of Parentage (*Nasab*)

The Prophet Muhammad (SAWS) is reported to have said, "The child is for the bed."[33] From this statement a general principle is laid down. A child, legitimate or illegitimate, always has a mother. The mother is the one who gives birth to it. Therefore, the surrogate mother will naturally, truly, and legally be the mother of the child. A child born under the surrogate contract would be illegitimate in the *Shari'ah* since the contracting husband had not entered into matrimonial contract with the surrogate mother who gave birth to the child.

There is no place for surrogate motherhood within the Islamic system, for the evils that would accrue from it will far outweigh any good. Some of its evils may be enumerated as follows. Acceptance of surrogate motherhood would:

1) tamper with the *Sunan* ("Ways") of Allah in the normal process of procreation;
2) entice unmarried women to "lease" their wombs for monetary benefits; this would in effect undermine the institution of marriage and family life;
3) tempt married women to resort to this technique in order to relieve themselves of the agony of going through the pangs of pregnancy and childbirth. Islam does not consider pregnancy as a burden but as a blessing. If a mother dies during pregnancy or childbirth she is given the status of *shahidah* ("martyr");
4) encourage the surrogate mother to claim legal rights to the couple's child she bore, as has already occurred in the United States; and
5) if not checked, create confusion in blood ties, when a mother like Pat Antony of Tzaneen, South Africa, carries the children of her biological daughter, Karen.[34]

It cannot be denied that biomedical science has made positive contributions towards assisting infertile couples in becoming parents. The technological methods used are sometimes ethically questionable. In the Islamic system ethics is not divorced from law. Thus, the question we have addressed is whether such techniques are valid under Islamic law? We have attempted to analyze all of the biotechnical possibilities and have come to the conclusion that only artificial insemination with the sperm of the husband (AIH) can be regarded as lawful.

The other functionally similar technique that could be looked upon as permissible would be *in vitro* fertilization where the ovum of the wife is fertilized by the sperm of the husband.

All other techniques cannot be legally sanctioned, for they involve an element of adulterous union and/or could destroy the institution of marriage.

The Qur'anic verse (42:50) stating that it is within the power of Allah (SWT) to leave barren whom He wills enables Muslims to resign themselves to the will of Allah (SWT) in the event that both the process of artificial insemination and *in vitro* fertilization fail and leave them without offspring.

If these two techniques fail, they have two further options. If the cause of infertility is the woman the husband may resort to polygamy and try to have children from his second wife. But, if they are so intimately attached to one another and would not like to be disturbed by the presence of another woman, even one legally married to the husband, then they have the option to adopt a child, preferably an orphan. Besides enjoying the spiritual benefits of this responsibility, they will also have the pleasure of rearing a child who may not legally be adopted by them but yet be psychologically satisfying to care for as if he or she were their own.

PART FOUR:
ABORTION

CHAPTER X
THE TERMINATION OF LIFE

Though abortion is today a very modern topic of considerable controversy, it has not been unknown in the annals of history. In fact, throughout the ages, some societies have permitted it and others prohibited it. For example, it is said that as far back as 2700 B.C. drugs were freely used in the Chinese society to induce abortion, while the Assyrian Code of 1500 B.C. condemned abortion in these words:

> Any woman who causes to fall what her womb holds.... shall be tried, convicted and impaled upon a stake, and shall not be buried.[1]

Abortion is the termination of pregnancy. It may be spontaneous as a result of physical injury to the woman or of some internal biomedical disorder or it may be deliberate through human intervention. Such intervention is by the use of certain drugs to terminate the pregnancy or by using a physician to end the pregnancy either by mechanically sucking out the contents of the uterus or by dilating the cervix and scraping its contents. If the pregnancy is in the advanced stage, other methods are employed. For example, the amniotic fluid surrounding the fetus may be removed and a solution of salt and water placed in its stead, which induces a miscarriage.[2]

Any abortion which occurs spontaneously as a result of internal biomedical factors is commonly known as a miscarriage. Such is not a matter of controversy. Ethics, law, and religion are concerned only with abortions that occur as a result of direct human intervention, whether self-inflicted or otherwise. These have religious, ethical, and legal implications.

From the above definition, it is to be understood that abortion is, in effect, any action undertaken with the aim of expelling the fetus inside the woman's womb before the end of the natural period of gestation.

I. SANCTITY OF LIFE

Islam, like other religions, upholds the sanctity of life. There are a number of verses in the Qur'an that testify to this. For example,

1) "And verily, we have honoured the Children of Adam" (17:70).
2) "If anyone slays a human being unless it be (in punishment) for murder or for spreading corruption on earth - it shall be as if he had slain the whole of mankind; whereas, if anyone saves a life, it shall be as if he had saved the lives of all mankind" (5:32).

   Moreover, there are other verses that emphatically warn against committing murder:

   3) "And do not take any human being's life - (the life) which Allah has willed to be sacred - otherwise than in (the pursuit of) justice" (17:33).
4) "Hence, do not kill your children for fear of want (poverty): it is We Who shall provide sustenance for them as well as for you. Verily, killing them is a great sin" (17:31).

   5) "And when the female infant, buried alive is questioned for what crime she was killed..." (81:8).

   Furthermore, it deplores suicide:

   "Do not kill yourselves: for verily Allah has been to you Most Merciful" (4:29).

Now let us analyse the implications of the above-mentioned verses. Verses 2) and 3) explicitly state that human life is sacred and therefore cannot be disposed of except for a just cause, that is, in the execution of a legal sentence, or in a just war, or in legitimate self-defence.[3] Verses 4) and 5) refer to the custom that was prevalent in pre-Islamic Arabia, namely *Wa'd*, which meant burying female infants alive.[4] The last verse refers to the taking of one's own life (i.e. suicide) which is a grave sin in Islam.[5] The first verse sums up the message of the Qur'an on the sanctity of human life.

Although all the above-mentioned verses do have direct bearing on the sanctity of human life as a whole, there are no Qur'anic verses directly on the issue of abortion. Nonetheless, the general teachings of the Qur'an and the *Sunnah* clearly establish that life in whatever form is to be preserved and is not to be destroyed except for a valid cause or reason. Thus in his address to the Muslim army before dispatching it to Syria, the first *khalifah* in Islam, Abu Bakr, gave the following order:

> Do not commit misappropriation or fraud, do not be guilty of disobedience (to the commander) and mutilation (of the limbs of any person). Do not kill old men, women, or children. Injure not the date-palm, nor burn it with fire; and cut not down

> the fruit-bearing trees. Slaughter not the sheep or cows or camels except for purposes of food....[6]

Muslims understand this prohibition as extending to all other forms of life, which may be killed only for a legitimate cause. We shall now look at the circumstances or reasons that, legally speaking, permit the termination of human life.

II. PERMITTED TERMINATION OF LIFE

Islam maintains that Allah (SWT) is the Sole Sovereign and Lawgiver and that the Qur'an is the Code of Conduct that should serve to regulate the lives of all mankind. At the same time, Islam holds that the Prophet Muhammad (SAWS) was endowed by Allah (SWT) with interpretive powers that in any other society would be considered legislative. The following Qur'anic verse elucidates this point clearly:

> We have revealed unto thee (Muhammad) the Remembrance (of the Qur'an) that you may explain to mankind that which has been revealed for them (16:44).
> And whatsoever the Messenger (Muhammad) gives you, take it. And whatsoever he forbids, abstain from it (59:7).

Commenting on these verses, Dr Muhammad Mustafa Azami, Professor of the Science of *Hadith*, University of Riyadh, says:

> These are some of the many Qur'anic verses which state the authority of the Prophet and emphasize the fact that his whole life, decisions, judgements and commands have binding authority and ought to be followed in all spheres of life by Muslim individuals and communities as well as Muslim States.[7]

Crimes in Islam encompass all actions contrary to the teachings of the Qur'an and *Sunnah* of the Prophet (SAWS). It is precisely for the sake of curtailing crimes and ensuring peace, security, and tranquility that Islam prescribes preventive and just punishments for acts that injure life without reasonable justification.[8] The basis of such penal laws is to be found in the Qur'an itself.[9] The termination of human life has been sanctioned by Allah (SWT) and the Prophet (SAWS) as a form of punishment for the following specific crimes:

A. Highway Robbery

> The punishment for those who wage war against God and His Apostle, and strive with might and main for mischief through the land is: execution, or crucifixion, or the cutting off of hands and feet from opposite sides, or exile from the land: that is their disgrace in this world, and a heavy punishment is theirs in the Hereafter (5:36).

Dr Ahmad Fathi Bahnasi explains the various ways in which the punishments stipulated in the above verse for highway robbers are to be carried out. He states that if the highway robber committed murder along with the theft of money or goods, then such a criminal is to be executed and thereafter crucified. If, however, only murder was committed without stealing anything, then the criminal is to be executed and be exempted from crucifixion. In the event that no act of murder took place but the criminal was guilty of theft, then such criminal's right hand and left leg are to be amputated. If, however, the highway robber only frightened the travellers but committed no act of murder nor theft, then such a criminal is to be exiled from the land.[10] There is no doubt that the explanation of Dr. Bahnasi serves in our understanding of the different forms of punishments that the Qur'an lays down for the ones guilty of the crime of highway robbery along with other crimes. These punishments may seem severe but the underlying purpose is to serve as a deterrent to such crimes.

B. Adultery

The Qur'anic verse on the punishment for illicit sexual intercourse is:

> The woman and the man guilty of indulging in illicit sexual intercourse, flog each of them with a hundred stripes... (24:2).

Prophet Muhammad (SAWS) is reported to have elucidated the above verse in the following manner:

> Take it from me. Take it from me. Verily Allah has chalked out a way for them. The (punishment for) fornication of a person with another person is a hundred stripes and exile for one year. And the (punishment for) committing of adultery of a married person to a married person is one hundred stripes and stoning to death.[11]

Dr. Abd al Qadir 'Awdah commenting on the punishment for illicit sexual intercourse states that lashing is the standard punishment for such an offence and, though the punishment of stoning to death is not explicitly found in the Qur'an, Prophet Muhammad (SAWS) interpreted the law by stating that the adulterer and adulteress besides being lashed must be stoned to death.[12]

C. Spreading Dissension or Discord

The punishment for such an offence, the Qur'an states, is as follows:

> If two parties among the Believers fall into a quarrel, make you peace between them: but if one of them transgresses beyond bounds against the other then fight you (all) against the one that transgresses until it complies with the command of Allah (49:9).

Dr. Bahnasi is of the opinion that this crime encompasses transgression against the leader (*Imam*) in pursuit of conspiracy to overthrow him and opposing the consensus of the majority while segregating oneself from the majority with the aim of spreading mischief within the community.[13] Spreading dissension and discord within the community is tantamount to disturbing internal peace and security, which could lead to anarchy and corruption. For people indulging in such a crime or crimes the Qur'an envisages that they should be fought, which implies that they are to be killed.

D. Apostasy

Apostasy is the renunciation or abandonment of Islam by one who professes the Islamic faith. Apostasy may be committed in belief, word, or deed, or even by wilfully conscientious and public repudiation of the obligatoriness or of the truthfulness of the bligatory practices.[14]

Speaking about the Muslim who apostatizes, the Qur'an states:

> And if any of you turn back from their faith and die in unbelief, their works will bear no fruit in this life and in the Hereafter; they will be companions of the Fire and will abide therein (2:217).

In this regard it is reported that the Prophet (SAWS) said: "Whoso changes his religion, kill him."[15] Only when a Muslim apostatizes and does not repent for this crime is he or she to be killed, according to the jurists.[16] The *Shari'ah* does hold all humans free to choose, or follow, any religion. But being a Muslim and residing in an Islamic society and publicly apostatising is tantamount to repudiating one's political affiliation with the *Ummah* or Islamic community. It is thus recognized as treason and therefore merits the death penalty.

E. Murder or Homicide

The Qur'anic punishment laid down for the willful murderer is as follows:

> O you who believe! Just retribution is ordained for you in cases of killing: the free for the free, and the slave for the slave, and the women for the women... (2:178).

The Arabic equivalent for the punishment of murder is *al Qisas* (just retribution). Commenting on it, Abdullah Yusuf Ali states: "Since one life has been lost, other lives should not be wasted in retaliation. At most, the law should take one life under strictly prescribed conditions and in this way the door to private vengeance or tribal retaliation would be shut."[17] Thus, if the death sentence is to be carried out in the case of murder, only the one guilty of the crime will be executed.

F. *Jihad* (Just War)

The Qur'an sanctions waging a just war in the following words:

> And fight them on until there is no more tumult or oppression, and there prevail justice and faith in Allah. But if they cease, let there be no hostility except to those who practice oppression (2:193).

Engaging in war necessarily implies that blood will be shed. But the above verse clearly stipulates that it should aim at putting a stop to oppression, which may take the form of persecution and hostility. As soon as that is achieved, peace should prevail.

From the teachings of Islam, it can therefore be deduced that life, in whatever form, is to be respected, nurtured, and allowed to follow the natural course of its evolution until its destined end. Life can be terminated only under strict provisions laid down in the Qur'an and *Sunnah* of the Prophet (SAWS).

CHAPTER XI

THE STATUS OF THE FETUS

When a woman becomes pregnant she is not looked upon as someone inflicted with an illness or a disease. Rather people extend congratulations to her. This is because after conception a "new life" is in the offing. This "new life" is not referred to by he prospective parents as the embryo or the fetus, as men of science and doctors do, but as their child. For already they have great expectation that this "new life" will be a person to grow up with them.[1]

Here is where the problem arises. Daniel Ch. Overduin aptly puts it in the following manner:

> The dilemma in the abortion debate is created by a number of relevant questions to which a host of different answers are given. These questions may relate to the humanity of the unborn; the right of the unborn; the future of the unborn in terms of physical, mental and social health; and the wishes, circumstances, and rights of the mother and father, people, and their world.[2]

Part of the problem is in defining the word "fetus." The word fetus, whose equivalent in the Arabic language is *janin* (pl. *ajinnah*), literally stands for anything veiled or covered.[3] From this definition, the *janin* or fetus would comprise anything that is developing inside the mother's womb from the time of conception until birth. At least one verse of the Qur'an makes mention of ajinnah (pl. of *janin*):

> He (Allah) knows you well when He brings you out of the earth, and when you are hidden (*ajinnah*) in your mothers' wombs (53:32).

Technically speaking, however, "science" maintains that the unborn is a fetus in the stage from eight weeks until birth, from which point in time (eight weeks) the fetus would be in possession of all the necessary human characteristics.[4]

Muslim scholors use three different definitions. Some maintain simply that the fetus stands for that which is in the womb.[5] Others, including Imam al Shafi'i, hold that the stage of "fetus" (*janin* or that which is in the womb) begins only when the stages of *al mudghah* (a chewed lump) and *al 'alaqah* (something that clings) have been completed and it can clearly be made out to be a human possessing differentiated characteristics, such as fingers, nails, or eyes.[6] The third group, represented by al Nuwayri, use the word *janin* (fetus) for that which exists in the womb after ensoulment has taken place.[7]

The Qur'anic reference to the fetus is general in nature. The Qur'an, refers to the procreated being inside the woman's body as *janin* (fetus) irrespective of the stage of its development, and this is the basic definition in Islamic law. Imam Shafi'i's definition, however, is helpful in that it is closest to modern scientific usage and reflects references in both the Qur'an and the *Hadith* to stages of fetal growth.

I. STAGES OF FETAL GROWTH

A. Scientific Analysis

Science maintains that the life of any particular person goes through stages in a continuum from the time of conception to death. There are four stages in the prenatal development of a human. The first is in the fallopian tube. This is the stage of the zygote, which is the female ovum (egg) that has been fertilized by the male sperm in the fallopian tube of the woman, where it remains for about three days. During this time, cell division begins. The stage of blastocyst starts with implantation in the uterus, where rapid cell division in the blastocyst continues. Many zygotes never attach, of course, and pass unnoticed through the woman's menses. The stage of the embryo begins two weeks after conception. At this time there is organ differentiation. All the internal organs one will ever have are present in rudimentary form by the end of six weeks. The procreated being is termed a fetus in the period from eight weeks to birth, during which stage there is continuous growth or development but nothing "new is added." This is the period of bringing to readiness for birth what has already begun.[8]

B. Qur'anic Analysis

The main Qur'anic passages referring to fetal growth are as follows:

> We created man from the quintessence of mud. Thereafter We caused him to remain as a drop of sperm (*nutfah*) in a firm lodging (i.e. the womb). Thereafter We fashioned the sperm into something that clings (*'alaqah*), which We fashioned into a chewed lump (*mudghah*). The chewed lump is fashioned into

> bones which are then covered with flesh. Then we nurse him into another act of creation (*khalqan akhar*). Blessed is Allah the Best of Creators (23:13).

> O men! If you are in doubt as to the resurrection, remember that We have created (everyone of) you out of dust, then out of a drop of semen (*nutfah*), then from something that clings (*'alaqah*), then from a leech-like lump (*mudghah*) (complete in itself), and yet incomplete (*ghayr mukhallaqah*) so that We might make (Our signs) clear unto you. We cause to rest whatever We want in the womb until the time We decide to bring you forth as infants (22:5).

C. *Hadith* Analysis

There are at least two significant *ahadith* that make direct reference to fetal development. They are:

> Each of you is constituted in your mother's womb for forty days as a *nutfah*, then it becomes an *'alaqah* for an equal period, then a mudghah, then an angel is sent, and he breathes the soul into it.[9]

> When forty-two nights have passed over the sperm drops, Allah sends an angel to it, who shapes it and makes its ears, eyes, skin, flesh and bones. Then, he says, "O Lord! Is it a male or female? And your Lord decides what He wishes and the angel records it.[10]

Now let us understand these various stages as enumerated in the Qur'an and Hadith literature. *Nutfah* literally means "a drop of fluid." Dr Maurice Bucaille emphasizes this point by stating that the Qur'an makes it clear that the fertilizing capacity of the sperm does not depend on the volume of liquid "poured out."[11] *'Alaqah* literally means "something that clings and adheres to the womb," clearly describing the implantation stage,[12] i.e., of the fertilized ovule in the uterus.[13] *Mudghah* literally means "a piece of flesh that has been chewed." Dr. al Bar says that the Qur'an depicts this stage as if it were a piece of flesh or food that has been chewed.[14]

We may recapitulate here that in the first *hadith* above, direct reference is made to the ensoulment of the fetus after 120 days from the time of fertilization. At the same time, some of the *mufassirun* (commentators on the Qur'anic text) hold that the words *khalqan akhar* (i.e., "another act of creation") at the end of the first Qur'anic passage quoted above signify the ensoulment of the fetus;[15] and that the stage of *mudghah ghayr mukhallaqah* (i.e., the lump not yet completely created) in the second Qur'anic passage denotes the stages "when no soul had yet been breathed into it."[16] It is noteworthy that the second *hadith* states that organ differentiation occurs forty-two nights after fertilization.

II. RIGHTS OF THE FETUS

The rights of the fetus and Islamic duties toward it are discussed below in general, i.e., without reference to its stage; and the word fetus is used in its wider connotation, signifying anything developing inside the mother's uterus after fertilization has taken place.

A. Right to Life

Besides what has already been mentioned above on the general sanctity of life as propounded by the Qur'an, Islamic law stipulates that the fetus has the right to life. This can be emphasized by the fact that all the Schools of Islamic law require postponement of the death penalty for a pregnant woman until after she has given birth and provisions have been made for the child to be suckled by a wet nurse.[17] Moreover, Ibn Qudamah mentions that the Shafi'i School makes provision for cutting the belly of the dead pregnant mother to remove the fetus, if there is any sign that the fetus is alive[18] (today it would be in the form of the Caesarian operation).

B. Inheritance

Islamic Law maintains that as long as the fetus is still inside its mother's womb, it does not enjoy the right of inheritance as such. Hence, if the testator passes away while the fetus is unborn, then the division of the inheritance should be postponed until after its birth.[19] This is so because there is no real guarantee that it will be born alive. If it is stillborn then it has no right in the inheritance.[20] Likewise, under normal circumstances, since one does not know whether the fetus will be born as a male or as a female, it is proper to await its birth before alloting its share from the inheritance, bearing in mind that there are special rules governing the shares to be alloted to the males and the females.

C. Burial of the Fetus

Islamic law states that the miscarried fetus or the stillborn fetus is to be buried. Ibn 'Abidin points out that a fetus that does not utter a sound at the moment of birth should be given the ceremonial bath (*al ghusl*), named, and placed in a piece of cloth (*kaffan*) and buried, but no prayer should be read over it. This, he maintains, applies to both the formed and unformed fetuses.[21]

The fetus is very much a person in all the teachings of Revelation. Islamic Law upholds the fetus's right to life. The requirement that the division of the inheritance be postponed until after the fetus's birth shows that due consideration is given to its existence. And the provision laid down for its burial after its death denotes that its sanctity is fully recognised.

CHAPTER XII

UNWANTED PREGNANCIES

In modern Western countries, abortion is sought most urgently as a result of illegitimate sex, rape, and the prospect of deformed fetuses. We shall examine each of these three cases to determine whether abortion in such cases can be justified.

I. ILLEGITIMATE SEX

There is no doubt that the sexual instinct is one of the strongest instincts in man. Dr Muhammad Fazl-ur-Rahman Ansari, describing this instinct, rightly says that its immediate goal is sexual union with an individual of the opposite sex, and its ultimate end is the procreation of the species.[1] It is precisely for the sake of channelling this instinct in the proper direction that the Prophet Muhammad (SAWS) admonished the young people, saying, "Young men, those of you who can support a wife should marry, for it keeps you from looking at women (lit., lowers your gaze) and preserves your chastity; but those who cannot should fast, for it is a means of cooling the sexual passion."[2] Thus, it can be said that in Islam, like other religions, the institution of marriage serves to legalize the sexual union. Today, however, marriage as the time for first sexual union has become somewhat outdated in the West and premarital sex seems to be the norm. This point was brought out by a report published in the *Sunday Times*, Durban, May, 1984, on a survey of British women. It stated:

> Virginity is right out of fashion, according to British women - and even church-going teenagers reckon it is O.K. to make love before marriage.[3]

Often these teenagers are not well informed about precautionary measures and the result is an increase in teenage pregnancies. In most of these cases, abortion is chosen as the solution to avoid premature parenthood. The following may not be such an extreme case:

> A ten-year old girl begins to show signs of pregnancy. A thoughtful and concerned social worker discovered that the girl was pregnant by her grandfather who lived with the family.

> After talking about and weighing various alternatives, the girl requested abortion. Her parents agreed and the social worker made the arrangements. After the abortion, the girl returned to her childhood routines, her life unaccompanied by a life-threatening pregnancy and her future unhindered by the prospect of premature parenthood.[4]

The Islamic solution to pregnancies from illegitimate sex does not favor abortion because this would be only a temporary solution. Islam condemns illegitimate sex and considers it a crime. The real solution is to eradicate or reduce such crime in society.

> Islam recognizes the strength and importunity of sex but it tries to satisfy the sexual instinct through legal means, i.e., marriage. Therefore, Islam advocates early marriage and provides aid from the public treasury for those who wish to get married yet cannot afford to do so. On the other hand, Islam purifies society from temptations that excite the passions. It also prescribes lofty and noble ideals which exhaust excessive vitality and direct it into the service of public interest. It prefers that leisure time should be spent in trying to become closer and closer to God. In this manner Islam eradicates all motives that lead to crime.[5]

Islam not only condemns illegitimate sex but dictates that persons guilty of such a crime should be publicly punished. The punishment, in itself, is severe and serves as a deterrent to such a crime. An incident from the lifetime of the Prophet Muhammad (SAWS) sheds light on the Islamic stand against abortion as an option in the event of pregnancy resulting from illegitimate sex:

> There came to him (the Holy Prophet) a woman from Ghamid and said, "Allah's Messenger, I have committed adultery, so purify me." He (the Holy Prophet) turned her away. On the following day she said, "Allah's Messenger why do you turn me away? Perhaps you turn me away as you turned away Ma'iz. By Allah, I have become pregnant." He said, "Well, if you insist upon it, then go away until you give birth to (the child)." When she delivered she came with the child (wrapped) in a rag and said, "Here is the child whom I have given birth to." He (the Prophet) said, "Go away and suckle him until you wean him." When she had weaned her child she came to him (the Holy Prophet) with the child who was holding a piece of

> bread in his hand. She said, "Allah's Apostle, here he is. I have weaned him and he eats food." He (the Holy Prophet) entrusted the child to one of the Muslims and then pronounced punishment.[6]

From the above incident, it is evident that the life of the unborn is to be highly valued. The punishment was meted out only after the birth and weaning of the child. The woman's persistent request to be purified of the crime shows the emphasis Islam lays on accountability before Allah (SWT) for one's actions. Such deterrents to promiscuity do not address the problem of pregnancy as a result of illegitimate sex once it occurs.

The *hadith* cited above suggests that pregnancy as a result of illegitimate sex should be carried to term. But what if a 10-year old girl becomes pregnant, seduced, let us say, by a 16-year old neighbor? Should she be compelled to carry the pregnancy to term? Since Islam does not uphold adoption in the modern legal sense of giving up all rights to the child, she will not have this as an option after her child is born. Would it not be more practical to allow her to undergo an abortion thus enabling her to resort to her childhood routines? This would surely save her from premature parenthood and provide her an opportunity later on to marry someone and start a family. But then the question would arise whether it would be morally sound for her to keep her seduction and abortion secret from her prospective husband? All these are real problems and the author is in no position to provide definite answers. It would be reasonable to let the l0-year old girl undergo an abortion during the early stages of pregnancy. This would ensure a better prospect for her to enter into matrimony later on in adulthood. But would not this permission set a precedent that could be abused?

II. RAPE

Although rape in itself is a sexual crime, it is certainly unlike adultery and fornication in the sense that it is associated with force and violence.

The number of forcible rapes in the United States was estimated at 63,020 in 1977,[7] while the *Sunday Tribune* of Durban, November 1983, reported that it was then estimated that in a year 300,000 women in South Africa would be raped.[8] An article in the *Daily News*, Durban, of August 30, 1984, aptly sums up the reason for the increase in such a crime:

> Films portraying cruelty and extreme violence towards women sexually arouse nearly a third who watch them....Several researchers told the symposium that they found that repeated viewings of films such as "Friday the 13," and "The Texas Chain-

> saw Massacre" instilled in the minds of viewers reactions similar to those found in rapists.[9]

It is to be noted that pregnancy resulting from rape is very unlikely. Commenting on this, Mahkorn and Dolan state: "Of this past decade's growing medical literature on sexual assault, several investigations have documented the actual incidence of rape-related pregnancy. The findings of pregnancy vary from an incidence of none (0) to 2.2 percent of the victims involved. In four of the studies no pregnancies were documented. This included a large percentage of women at risk who for various reasons did not take any hormones such as DES."[10]

From the above, it is evident that pregnancy as a result of rape is most unlikely, but, at the same time, one cannot absolutely rule out the possibility of its occurrence. If pregnancy does occur from rape, one is confronted with the question whether abortion is justified. One would be inclined to answer that question in the affirmative in view of the fact that the sexual act was imposed upon the woman by force against her will and thus, it may be argued, the woman has every right not to want to carry the child of someone who has no emotional attachment to her. But deeper analysis of the problem of rape and pregnancy reveals that pregnancies that result from rape are those that are not reported. The victims of sexual assault are, in most cases, given due medical attention. Mahkorn and Dolan explained this in the following manner:

> Rape is both a psychological emergency and a medical emergency.... Therapeutic goals of these procedures include treatment of any physical injuries, crisis intervention with emotional support, prophylaxis for venereal disease, and medication for potential pregnancy.[11]

The Islamic solution to the problem of rape would be, first, to: call for an end to all forms of indecent exposure of the body in public; ban pornographic motion pictures, literature, and songs; curtail the free-intermingling of sexes; and stop the use of women as an enticement in advertisements to sell goods or products of any sort. Over and above this, we should demand that those guilty of committing such a heinous crime as rape should be publicly punished. If after taking all the above precautionary measures, rape does occur, then the victim should seek immediate medical attention for possible prevention of pregnancy. Medically speaking, immediately after the sexual act has taken place, as in the case of rape, it is not possible to establish whether pregnancy has occured. Hence, at that point in time it would be permissible to take medications against pregnancy. Al-Qurtubi holds the view that the semen is not something definite and certain (*yaqinan*), and that a woman may get rid of it before it settles in the womb.[12] If no steps are taken, however, to report the rape and obtain medical help against possible pregnancy, then apparently it would be unjustified to advocate an abortion after the lapse of many days or months, for then it would be difficult to establish medically whether rape had in reality taken place. And this may lead to abuse.

Creating an Islamic environment whereby the society would be purged of all forms of temptations so as to ensure the non-occurrence of all forms of rape is no doubt commendable. But this can in no way guarantee the non-occurrence of rape. There will always be exceptions to the rule. It is true that the strict laws envisaged by Islam for those guilty of fornication and adultery could serve as a deterrent against rape. But such laws can be enforced only by a Muslim government. Thus, advocating the implementation of such laws as a possible deterrent to rape would not solve the problem, because such laws would never be implemented in non-Muslim countries. Even in the Muslim World, aside from Saudi Arabia and Iran and to an extent Pakistan, they are not upheld.

Second, if every woman were to seek immediate medical attention after being raped, then that would surely solve the problem of resorting to abortion to terminate any resulting pregnancy. But, in Muslim countries or environments, fear of ostracism makes it difficult for victims to report the rape. Ostracizing such women is certainly un-Islamic, but the tendency exists to look down upon them, so even their chances of getting married would be jeopardized. Hence, concern about what to do generally arises only after pregnancy has been confirmed, at which time it is impossible to establish medically whether rape in reality did take place.

The question then arises whether it is fair to either mother or child for the child to be carried to term. Joseph Fletcher argues that the governing ethical principle should be pregnancy by choice and certainly not by compulsion.[13] To insist that she has to continue the pregnancy would surely contradict the earlier position against artificial insemination by a donor (A.I.D.). It was argued that the issue of donor sperm would be illegitimate and therefore not an acceptable means of overcoming infertility. In the case of pregnancy as a result of rape the child would also be illegitimate.

It may sometimes happen that a married woman is raped while her husband is in another country, perhaps on business. Would he want his wife to bear the child of another man? Indeed, the woman herself would not be comfortable to carry to term the child of someone who inflicted upon her such a traumatic experience. These are all genuine problems. The author is inclined to hold that in the case of pregnancy as a result of rape, abortion should be justified. But would that be just? After all, the fetus committed no crime. How then could its life be terminated?

III. DEFORMITIES

With the advances in modern biomedical technology, prenatal diagnoses can today be carried out safely and with considerable accuracy. The techniques used for such diagnoses may be enumerated as follows:

1) Amniocentecis
2) Fetoscopy
3) Ultrasound, and
4) X-rays[14]

Nowadays, Muslim jurists are confronted with the question whether abortion can be permitted if there is:

1) A risk of genetically transmitted disease;
2) Evidence of a congenital defect;
3) An intra-uterine diagnosis of a severe fetal abnormality incompatible with life.

In reply to the questionnaire sent to the *Dar al Ifta* in Riyadh, Saudi Arabia, on such issues by the Islamic Medical Association of South Africa, it was categorically stated in the religious decree (*fatwa*) that abortion on such grounds cannot be permitted.[15] Although Islamic teachings require all necessary steps to protect society from defective newborns, resort to abortion of deformed fetuses can never be justified. Rather, knowledgeable scholars emphasize the need to solve the problem by going to its root.

Specific forms of deformity most commonly encountered are drug-induced mental retardation, Down's Syndrome, and genetic disease.

A. Mental Retardation

Professor Ali Musa, Head of the Department of Paediatrics, University of Natal, Durban, South Africa, in his paper on "The Fetal Alcohol Syndrome," affirms that:

> Most infants with the fetal alcohol syndrome are mentally retarded....[16]

The best solution to this problem is absolute prohibition of drinking alcohol.[17]

Moreover, it is now established that a child born to a mother who is infected with STD (sexually transmitted disease) may lose its eyesight or suffer brain damage. The *Sunday times Magazine*, Durban, May 1985, reports:

> Babies are the most pitiful victims of the sexual revolution. A

> child born to a mother who is known to be infected with one of about 25 types of sexually transmitted disease (STD) is assured of a traumatic time, even in its first hours of life. At best, its eyes may have to be treated immediately to prevent the possibility of eventual blindness.... At most, the newborn child may be suffering from neo-natal (and life-threatening) herpes, which can cause permanent brain damage in those infants who survive the disease.[18]

The solution to these problems is to condemn all acts that may in one way or the other lead to any sexual offence.[19]

B. Down's Syndrome

Dr Omar S. Alfi who has studied fetal deformity in Kuwaiti society discovered that:

> The frequency of a number of genetic disorders was significantly higher among offspring of consanguineous, as compared to non-consanguineous marriages. The most significant of these was the occurence of Down's Syndrome (Mongolism).[20]

It is generally accepted that Down's Syndrome is linked to two independent factors, namely, consanguinity as pointed out in Dr Alfi's paper, and advanced maternal age as discovered in researchs carried out in Canada.[21]

The Islamic solutions to this problem lie in the advice given by the Prophet Muhammad (SAWS), who admonished: "Marry from afar to avoid weak progeny,"[22] and, "Young men, those of you who can support a wife should marry"....[23]

C. Carriers of Genetic Disease

If it is established that the prospective partners are both carriers of a certain genetic disease and that their union may result in the transmission of that disease to their progeny, then some sort of counselling should be done to apprise them of the apparent risks involved. If both, in spite of that, are still willing to contract the marriage then it may be wise for them to use contraceptive devices to safeguard against the conception of children with the genetic disease. Imam al Ghazali makes a clear distinction between contraception and abortion.[24]

If, however, after taking all precautionary measures, deformed fetuses are detected, it would be best to consider this a trial from the Almighty and to practice patience, bearing in mind what the Qur'an says:

> Your riches and your children are but a trial: and in the presence of Allah is the highest reward.[25]

The religious decree issued by *Dar ul Ifta*, Riyadh, against the aborting of deformed fetuses may be appreciated if we bear in mind that the life-span of grossly deformed fetuses is naturally short. Monteleone and Moraczewski point out that:

> Anencephaly is lethal; many fetuses are aborted spontaneously, some are stillborn, and a few survive for a few hours or days.[26]

The proposed Islamic solutions for fetal deformity are indeed noble in the sense that they do not advocate the aborting of defective fetuses. Surely it is better to marry early to avoid Down's Syndrome and to avoid alcohol to reduce the chance of mental retardation. But what about deformity of the fetus from maternal rubella? If maternal rubella is contracted during the first trimester, the child may manifest certain malformations at birth. They may be in the form of cataracts, deafness, heart lesions, or dental defects.[27] Any woman, aware of such a fate for her child would surely be worried and this could aggravate her mental health. Only in very rare cases can a woman accept such news calmly, placing her trust in Allah (SWT) and accepting it as a trial from Him. Would advocating abortion in such a case be justified? Surely, it would relieve the woman of her mental anguish and prevent the child from starting its life as a handicapped person? But, as Hussey points out, "The truth of the matter is that there is still too much uncertainty regarding the risks induced by rubella in a pregnant woman."[28]

We cannot overlook the fact that the fate of deformed fetuses is indeed a highly complex problem. Advocating their prenatal abortion may in time come to lead to the justification of euthanasia for the handicapped and even old people, who are often viewed as gross burdens on society or on their families.

In the above-mentioned three cases of what may be termed unwanted pregnancies, abortion can never be an acceptable solution. There are clear Islamic solutions. In order to curtail the crimes of illegitimate sex and rape, we should instead direct our efforts to purify society of the temptations that lead to these crimes. Moreover, we should advocate severe punishment for the offenders as a deterrent to such crimes. To advocate abortion for pregnancies resulting from illegitimate sex or rape would be to advocate killing the innocent rather than punishing the guilty for their crimes.

The problem of deformed fetuses is addressed Islamically by taking precautionary measures to avoid the birth of defective children rather than by killing them. Taking the lives of these innocent persons is not an act of true mercy, but an act of oppression against them. Indeed with the advances being made in the field of biomedical technology there is a growing possibility of prenatal treatment for certain fetal deformities.

In analysing Islamic solutions to the problem of unwanted pregnancies we must be aware that the problems are complex in nature and that no solutions can be considered final. We still need deeper research into the problems.

CHAPTER XIII
WARRANT FOR ABORTION

As we have seen, the revelation of Allah (SWT), the *Sunnah* of is Prophet (SAWS), and the best reasoning of Islamic scholars do not condone abortion of fetuses on the ground that the pregnancies were unwanted. In this chapter we shall consider references made to abortion in the Islamic juridical and medical literature in order to determine what are the generally accepted reasons for abortion.

I. ABORTION IN ISLAMIC JURIDICAL LITERATURE

Mohammed Mekki Naciri states that all Islamic juridical literature of the various schools of Islamic Law unanimously hold abortion to be a blameworthy act and that it is permissible only if motivated by a worthwhile reason.[1] Dr. Yusuf al Qaradawi points out that all Muslim jurists hold abortion, after the ensoulment of the fetus, to be *haram* (i.e., forbidden) and a crime against a living and fully formed being.[2]

A. The Hanafi School

Ibn 'Abidin, one of the Hanafi scholars, states that permission to abort is subject to the validity of the reason. A valid reason for an abortion before the fourth month of pregnancy, he states, is a threat to the life of a nursing infant. The new pregnancy may interfere with lactation. In the event that there is no possibility of getting a wet-nurse to breast-feed the already existing infant, and the mother fears her baby will die,[3] she may abort the fetus to save the life of the existing infant.

B. The Maliki School

The view of this school on abortion is found in *Hashiyah al Dasuqi*. It is stated that it is not permissible to induce abortion once the semen has been retained in the womb, even during the first 40 days of pregnancy. After ensoulment, abortion is absolutely prohibited (*haram*).[4]

C. The Shafi'i School

Imam al Ghazali, one of the eminent scholars of this school, in his *Ihya 'Ulum al Din*, states that contraception is not like abortion or *Wa'd* (burying of the infant girl alive), because abortion is a crime against an existing being. Existence has stages. The first stages of existence are the settling of the semen in the womb and its mixing with the secretions of the woman. It is then ready to receive life. Disturbing it is a crime. When it acquires a soul and its creation is completed, the crime becomes grievous. The crime reaches maximum seriousness when it is committed after the fetus is separated from the mother alive.[5]

D. The Hanbali School

Ibn Qudamah, in his *al Mughni*, puts forth the view of this school by stating: "Whoever hits the belly of a pregnant woman causing an abortion must give the blood wit. Likewise, if the pregnant woman drinks a medicine that results in her aborting the fetus, she has to give the blood wit.[6]

Evidently the Hanafi school is the most flexible on abortion. It specifies that before the fourth month of pregnancy, an abortion may be induced if a woman's pregnancy poses a threat to the life of her already existing infant. The Maliki position prohibits an abortion after implantation has taken place, while the Shafi'i school maintains that at any stage after fertilization the zygote should not be disturbed, and interference with its development would be a crime. The Hanbali school by stipulating the payment of blood wit for causing a miscarriage shows that it regards abortion as a sin.

Of all the four positions, the Hanafi position is the most flexible because it leaves room for further interpretations to determine other reasons that could be considered valid for inducing an abortion. We have to admit, however, that until today no serious attempt has been made in this direction. The evidence for this is that Dr. al Buti, a modern scholar, is of the opinion that an abortion may be sanctioned in the following three cases before the fourth month of pregnancy: if the doctors fear that the mother's life is in danger as a result of the pregnancy; if the pregnancy might cause a disease in the body of the mother; and if the new pregnancy severely reduces the mother's production of milk (lactaction) and her already existing infant is absolutely dependent on its mother's milk for survival.[7] Dr. al Buti does not state anything new, but only repeats the earlier positions.

Although the mother's life takes precedence over that of the young fetus, the priorities change if the mother's life is in danger after the fourth month of pregnancy, because after the 120 day period Muslim jurists hold that ensoulment occurs. At this point in time the fetus has a right equal to its mother. But, this dilemma is resolved by the general principle of the *Shari'ah*: choosing the lesser of two evils. Rather than losing both lives, the life of one should be given preference over the other. Shaykh Shaltut in his *Fatawa* ruled that the mother's life in this case should be saved and the fetus should be aborted:

> For the mother is the origin of the fetus; moreover, she is established in life, with duties and responsibilities, and she is also a pillar of the family. It is not possible to sacrifice her life for the life of the fetus which has not yet acquired a personality and which has no responsibilities or obligations to fulfil.[8]

II. ABORTION IN THE WRITINGS OF CLASSICAL MUSLIM PHYSICIANS

Let us now analyze the position of the classical Muslim physicians on abortion. We know they did in fact perform abortions. Did they do so arbitrarily, or did they back their actions with some sort of medical reasons. Here are the views of some of the most prominent doctors:

Al Razi (d.923 A.C.)

Abu Bakr Muhammad ibn Zakariyya al Razi (Latinized as Rhazes) was born in 865 A.C. in Rayy in Persia. He was in charge of the hospitals in Rayy and Baghdad and, besides being a great physician, was a philosopher and alchemist.[9] Reference to abortion is found in his celebrated work *Kitab al Hawi*. Ascribing to Hippocrates his own justification for abortion, Razi states: "Hippocrates said: Abortive medicines should be used before childbirth in the event that the pregnant woman was a virgin who was prematurely deflowered and became pregnant while of tender age. Abortion of the fetus is to be carried out before it grows big; otherwise the pregnant woman would die. Any woman the condition of whose *os uteri* was such (that is, small) will die if the fetus were to reach full growth'."[10]

B. Ali Ibn Abbas (949-82 A.C.)

He was of Persian origin from a family of al-Ahwaz, and served as a physician to the Buwayhid prince, Adud al Dawlah Fana Khusrau. In his *Kitab Kamil al Sina'ah al Tibbiyyah,* he begins his discussion on abortion in the following manner: "As to medicines that prevent conception, although they should not be mentioned to prevent their use by women unnecessarily, it is necessary to prescribe them to those women who have a small pelvis or those who have a disease that in the case of pregnancy may cause the woman's death in childbirth. Except for women in such predicaments, the physicians should not prescribe (these) medicines. Also, he should not prescribe medicines that cause the menses to flow, or medicines that expel the dead fetus, except to women he can trust, because all these medicines kill the fetus and expel it."[11]

C. Ibn Sina (d. 1037 A.C.)

Abu Ali al Husayn ibn Abd Allah Ibn Sina (Avicenna in Latin) was born in Afshana near Bukhara in 980 A.C. He was well versed in the Qur'an, law, logic, metaphysics, mathematics, astronomy, and medicine.[12] In his famous work, *Kitab al Qanun*, he has the following to say in his introduction to the chapter on abortion: "At times it may be necessary to induce abortion: that is when the pregnant woman is young and small and it is feared that childbirth would cause her death, or when she suffers from a disease of the uterus or when a fleshy growth in the uterus makes it very difficult for the fetus to emerge. Also when the fetus dies in the womb of the woman."[13]

D. Ibn Hubal (d. 1213 A.C.)

Muhadhdhib al Din Abu al Hasan Ali Ahmad, popularly known as Ibn Hubal, was born in Baghdad in 1122 A.C. Though he began his studies in grammar and law, he soon shifted to medicine.[14] His chief work, *al Mukhtarat fi al Tibb*, advises that, "Contraceptive and abortive medicines should not be mentioned to the common people, but ought to remain restricted to the circles of physicians for them to use in certain cases whenever necessary."[15]

Being medical practitioners, these classical Muslim physicians could only advocate that an abortion be induced for thereapeutic reasons. Their positions cannot provide sufficient guidance for definitive positions on the issue, because they were limited to the realm of their professions only.

III. HAZARDS OF ABORTION

In addition to the above considerations on the ethically justified purposes of abortion, we must consider the inherent hazards.

A. Urological and Renal Complications

Richard A. Watson points out that, "Diverse and sometimes life-threatening urologic complications have been encountered in induced abortions performed in all three trimesters of pregnancy. Surgical intervention in the third trimester may result in injury to the bladder and ureters. Amnio-infusion in the second trimester may present a threat of mechanical damage to the bladder and a compromise of renal function, particularly in patients with pre-existing renal disease or hypertension. Dilation and curettage and vacuum aspiration may endanger the bladder and ureters in first trimester abortions; urinary incontinence and various urinary tract infections may result."[16]

B. Infertility and Miscarriages

Interruption of the pregnancy by abortion may lead to infertility in the sense that the woman may not be able to carry to term any future child. Matthew J. Bulfin records the following case study:

> A 16-year old patient underwent a saline abortion in 1972 at the urging of her mother. The saline abortion was painful and greatly protracted: it lasted 48 hours before the patient expelled the fetus. Complications of fever and endometritis developed, prolonging her hospital stay. The following year she married the boy who had impregnated her, but since then she has suffered three miscarriages and harbors deep resentment towards the mother.[17]

C. Maternal Mortality

Induced abortions may result in maternal mortality. Thomas W. Hilgers and Dennis O'Hare, in their study on "Abortion Related Maternal Mortality" concluded that the trend in maternal deaths due to induced abortion showed that while maternal deaths stemming from criminal abortion appear to be decreasing, they have been replaced, almost one for one, by maternal deaths due to legal abortion. And in comparing the relative risk of natural pregnancy versus that of legal abortion, natural pregnancy was found to be safer in both the first and second 20 weeks of pregnancy.[18]

CHAPTER XIV

PUNISHMENT FOR FETICIDE

Muslim jurists classify crimes under three distinct divisions: crimes against the total person, which aim at taking the life of that person, i.e., homicide; crimes aimed at certain parts of the body such as physical assault or injury; and crimes against what is both a person and a non-person. Under this latter category is aggression against the fetus, which is considered a person because of its human constitution and a non-person because it is still unseparated from its mother's body.[1] Though feticide is not homicide, any aggression against the fetus is considered a crime.

I. FORMS OF AGGRESSION AGAINST THE FETUS

Aggression against the fetus implies any action that leads to the termination of its life or to the separation of the fetus from its mother before the end of the normal period of pregnancy, whether the action is undertaken by the pregnant woman herself or by some one else. Aggression may take three forms: 1) the indirect form of a verbal rebuke or threat against the pregnant woman, 2) the direct form of intentional action designed to expel the fetus from the womb, or 3) the form of indirect action, i.e. action that directly results in a miscarriage but without prior intention. The following illustrate each of these forms:

A. Verbal Rebuke or Threat

Verbal rebuke or threat may be of such a nature that it creates within the pregnant woman a degree of fear that may cause her to have a miscarriage. For example someone may threaten to kill her or hurt her in one way or another.[2]

B. Direct Action

Direct action is when the pregnant woman uses certain drugs with the aim of terminating the pregnancy[3] or visits a physician with the intention of undergoing an abortion. A direct action occurs also when a person strikes the belly of a pregnant woman, as a result of which she miscarries and a dead fetus is expelled.[4]

C. Indirect Action

Indirect action is not particularly aimed at terminating the pregnancy but, nevertheless, has this result. This may be effected by the pregnant woman in one of several ways, e.g., by starving herself, by fasting, or by smelling something pungent.[5]

II. FORMS OF COMPENSATION

A. *Al Ghurrah*

Al ghurrah literally means a whiteness the size of a *dirham* on the forehead of a horse. In technical legal language, however, it refers to the compensation levied for the destroying of a child in the womb.[6]

Reference to *al ghurrah* is made in the *hadith* literature. For example, in the *Sahih al Bukhari*, Abu Hurayrah narrates that two women of the tribe of Hudhayl quarrelled. One of them threw a stone at the other causing her to have a miscarriage. The Apostle of Allah gave his verdict that the *ghurrah* (compensation) be given in the form of manumitting a male or female slave.[7]

On the basis of this *hadith* and other relevant *ahadith* referring directly to *al ghurrah*, the Muslim jurists conclude that the payment of *al ghurrah* is necessary for all three of the above mentioned kinds of aggression against the fetus.[8] Opinion differs, however, whether *ghurrah* is obligatory if the fetus is expelled from its mother's body while still in an unformed state.

Imam Malik holds that the *ghurrah* is to be paid even though the fetus is in an unformed state.[9] Imams Abu Hanifah and al Shafi'i are of the opinion that it is to be paid as long as whatever comes out of the woman's body can be made out to be the beginning of human creation.[10] According to the Hanbali school, if any act to terminate the pregnancy (such as taking certain medicines) is taken within 40 days of conception, the payment of *al ghurrah* is not necessary.[11]

It is said that the value of *al ghurrah* is equivalent to *nisf ushr*, which is 1/20 of the full *diyyah* (or compensation).[12] It may take the form of freeing a male or female slave of the best quality, as mentioned above in the *hadith* of Abu Hurayrah in *Sahih al Bukhari*,[13] or of one hundred sheep, as recorded in the *hadith* of Abu Buraydah in *Sunan al Nasa'i*,[14] or of five hundred dirhams in cash, as pointed out in the *hadith* of *al Sha'bi* in *Sunan Abu Daud.*[15] Sayyid Sabiq adds that its payment may also be made in the form of five camels.[16]

As indicated above, feticide may be committed directly by the pregnant woman herself or indirectly by someone else whose action, such as assault and battery, against her unintentionally causes the death of the fetus.

The Hanafi and Shafi'i Schools hold that the *ghurrah* should be paid by the family on the father's side of the pregnant woman if she kills the fetus herself, or by the family of the person who indirectly, i.e., unintentionally, causes her to miscarry.[17] In the second case, the person is not himself or herself personally responsible for payment of the *ghurrah* because it cannot be proven that the miscarriage or death of the fetus took place as a result of his or her hostile action, and because the hostile action or aggression was not aimed directly against the fetus but, rather, at the pregnant woman.[18]

The Hanbali School, however, points out that if both fetus and mother die, and the aggression against the mother was a mistake or semi-intentional, then full compensation (for the dead mother), as well as the *ghurrah*, are due from the family of the aggressor. But if the hostile action against the mother was deliberate or intentional, or if the fetus alone dies, the family of the aggressor is not responsible to pay anything. Instead it is the duty of the aggressor alone to pay the *ghurrah.*[19]

The Maliki School is of the opinion that the aggressor personally, not his family, is responsible for paying the *ghurrah*, because the miscarriage of the fetus as a result of a blow on the pregnant woman's belly was not deliberate. The aggression was intentional as regards the pregnant woman but a mistake as regards the fetus.[20]

Ibn Rushd states that Imams Shafi'i and Abu Hanifah are of the opinion that the heirs (relatives) of the fetus should be the ones to benefit from *al ghurrah*. The rules pertaining to *al ghurrah* and *al diyyah* (blood money) are the same, in that both are inherited. Rabi'ah and al Laith, however, hold that the sole beneficiary should be the mother (of the aborted or miscarried fetus) since it (the fetus) is part and parcel of its mother's body.[21]

The discussion on *al ghurrah* is summarized in *Mughni al Muhtaj* in the following manner:

> There is no difference in the aggressor (against the fetus) being a foreigner or the pregnant woman herself. But if necessity calls upon her to use certain medicines, then as Zarkashi says, she is not held responsible for its cause (which may result in a miscarriage). It is not necessary for her to fast though it be in the month of Ramadan if she fears that a miscarriage might occur. So if she does fast and it results in her having a miscarriage then she is to be held responsible as al Mawardi said

> and she cannot inherit from the *ghurrah* for she is (held as) the killer (of the fetus).[22]

Ibn Qudamah is of the view that if a pregnant woman takes a medicine and a miscarriage results, she has to pay the *ghurrah* and she has no right to inherit from it.[23]

B. The *Diyyah Kamilah* (Full Blood Money)

As we have seen, Muslim jurists hold that the fetus is ensouled after the fourth month of pregnancy, on the basis of the directly relevant *hadith* of the Prophet Muhammad (SAWS). Hence, it follows that any act of aggression against the fetus after the fourth month would be tantamount to taking the life of a human being. Thus the aggressor would be liable to pay the *diyyah kamilah* (the full blood money) in compensation, and not the *ghurrah*.[24] The Hanbali School holds, however, that only if the fetus is separated from its mother's body during the sixth month of pregnancy is the *diyyah kamilah* due instead of the *ghurrah*. This school does not deny that ensoulment does take place after the fourth month of pregnancy, but its criterion for determining the time when the full blood money is due as a result of an aggression against the fetus is not the ensoulment but rather the viability of the fetus. This, it holds, can only be when the fetus is in its twenty-fourth week.[25]

All four schools of Islamic Law are of the opinion that any aggression against the fetus would be classified as semi-intentional if the aggressor deliberately intended the act, and a mistake if it was not deliberate.[26] Thus, the basis for the necessity of paying the *diyyah kamilah* is the following verse of the Qur'an:

> Never should a believer kill a believer, but (if it so happens) by mistake, (compensation is due): If one so kills a believer, it is ordained that he should free a believing slave and pay a compensation (*diyyah*) to the deceased's family....(4:92).

Payment of the *diyyah kamilah* may be made to the deceased's family in the form of one hundred camels, or two hundred cattle, or two thousand sheep, or one thousand *dinars*, or twelve thousand *dirhams*.[27] If the pregnant woman herself is the aggressor, then she will be liable to pay the full blood compensation to the heirs of the fetus, and she herself would not have any share in it.

C. *Al Kaffarah*

In the above verse it is explicitly stated that, besides the compensation one has to give to the family of the deceased as a result of having wrongfully killed another believing person, one has also to free a believing slave. This is one of many penalties designed gradually to eliminate the entire institution of slavery. This act is termed *kaffarah*, which means penance or atonement (for a sin).[28] In the event that no slave is found then the Qur'an stipulates that one should fast (instead) for two consecutive months.[29]

The Shafi'i School and the Hanbali School[30] hold that the *kaffarah* is necessary for any aggression against the fetus, along with the payment of the *diyyah kamilah*. The Hanafi School, however, says that only if the fetus is separated from its mother's body alive and then dies as a result of the aggression (against it) would the *kaffarah* be compulsory,[31] but does not make it a necessary obligation on the one who has committed an aggression against the fetus.[32]

The *kaffarah* in our contemporary time would be fasting for two consecutive months, as stated earlier. This creates a problem: What if someone has started to fast and falls ill before completing the required fasts? And what is the obligation of women who menstruate once every month, since menstruation in itself exempts one from keeping fasts, legally speaking? Al Jassas solves this dilemma by suggesting that the one who falls ill during the two month period should start all over again after he or she is well. Hence, the days already fasted would not be counted when the person concerned renews the fast. This is so, he explains, because sickness in itself does not nullify the fast and in the event that one does not fall ill it is possible to keep the fast for two months consecutively. But the woman who misses some of the fasts as a result of menstruation can add the days fasted to those that she would fast after the termination of the menstruation. Thus she does not have to start all over again, for it is a fact that any woman would normally menstruate each month (before she reaches the age of menopause). Al Jassas explains that the reason for this is that menstruation necessarily nullifies the fast (and as much as a woman would like to continue with the fast, legally speaking, she would not be able to do so). So, just as the night (wherein one cannot legally keep the fast) does not interrupt the consecutive days of the fasts, in the same way, menstruation would not interrupt the sequence of the consecutive fasts if the fasts missed as a result of the menstruation are made up immediately after the termination of the menstruation.[33]

Dr 'Abd al Qadir 'Awdah is of the opinion that all persons who are involved in the aggression against the fetus should share in the payment of the *diyah*, and likewise each of them should make the *kaffarah*.[34]

The question arises whether the Muslim doctor involved in carrying out the abortion is liable to share in the *diyah* and *kaffarah*? Ibn Rushd states that the Muslim jurists unanimously hold a doctor responsible for any mistake he or she may commit. But the *diyah* or compensation for the mistake is to be paid by the family on the paternal side of the doctor and not from the wealth of the doctor, for the mistake was unintentional.[35] Participation of a Muslim doctor in the act of inducing an abortion would make him or her responsible, unless the abortion is for therapeutic reasons, because abortion, as stated earlier, is a crime. Therefore if he or she induces the abortion after the fourth month (i.e., after ensoulment has taken place) for non-therapeutic reasons, he or she would be liable to pay a share in the *diyah kamilah* and expected to atone for his or her role in it by fasting for two consecutive months (as *kaffarah*). If he or she carries out the abortion for non-therapeutic reasons before the fourth month then he or she should pay the *ghurrah* in compensation.

It is clear that in Islamic thought feticide is not included in the crime of homicide. Nevertheless, it is considered a crime and the *Shari'ah* prescribes certain punishments for anyone guilty of an aggression against the fetus, whether the act is deliberately aimed at killing the fetus as in the case of abortion, as we know it today, or if the act is not aimed at the fetus directly, as in the case of striking the belly of a pregnant woman, but nevertheless, results in the death of the fetus through miscarriage. The different schools of Islamic law do indeed differ in the punishments to be meted out for feticide. But the differences of opinion among them are of no major consequence. The important thing is that all the schools hold feticide to be a crime and are in agreement that the punishments should take the form of either *al ghurrah* or *diyah kamilah*, with the *kaffarah* depending on the stage of fetal development at the time of the aggression.

CONCLUSION

Now that we have explored the technological details and related ethical nuances of reproductive control, biotechnical parenting, and abortion, we should stand back and "look at the forest" as distinct from its individual trees. Our exploration has revealed the intensity of the problems these issues pose. Each of these issues, in one way or another, is directly linked to the question of human life.

Reproductive control, calls for certain precautionary measures to frustrate the very possibility of pregnancy, and aims at the prevention of the birth of human beings from the very outset, prior to conception. Abortion actually terminates human life after conception and implantation. Biotechnical parenting, on the other hand, offers technological measures designed to help infertile couples have children and perpetuate the human race.

Analysis of the ethical issues in bio-medical technology should be derived from the guidance of Allah, Who alone has absolute knowledge of good and bad. In a beautiful passage mentioning the different stages of embryonic development, the Qur'an reveals that every person is created by Alllah:

> Man we did create from a quintessence of clay, then we placed him as a drop of sperm in a place of rest, firmly fixed. Then we made the sperm into a clot of congealed blood; then that clot we made a lump; then we made out of that lump bones and clothed the bones with flesh; then we developed out of it another creature, so blessed be Allah, the Best to create (23:12-14).

The husband and wife engage in the sexual act so the sperm can fertilize the ovum and begin human life. But it is Allah (SWT) Who in reality blesses some human beings with children while others He chooses to leave barren.

This has raised the question whether biomedical measures to increase or restore fertility constitute interference with Allah's *sunan* (Ways). This seeming dilemma is addressed by understanding that infertility should be viewed as a "disease." Since the Prophet (SAWS) emphasized that his followers should seek medical aid or attention whenever the need arises, it logically follows that trying to resolve infertility through modern biotechnological means would not be tantamount to denying one's trust in

Allah (SWT).

Nevertheless, we have seen that some of the biotechnical means may not be legitimate under the *Shari'ah*, for example, artificial insemination by a third party (AID) and surrogate parenting. Only two means are morally legitimate, namely, artificial insemination by the husband (AIH) and in vitro fertilization. Since these two techniques may not prove successful in resolving the problem of infertility, if both fail then Muslims have the option of adopting children who remain legally the children of their biological parents but are raised by the adopting couple as their own children.

Man was created to know and serve Allah (SWT). In the Qur'an Allah announced, "I have not created man and jinn except to serve me" (51:56). Man is entrusted to realize the *summum bonum* as evealed by Him. Moreover, the Qur'an affirms that the world was not created in vain (3:191). The world is the arena in which man is to prove his worth by realizing the ethical ideal. Because of his unique ethical vocation and destiny man is higher than the angels and is the crown of creation.[1] Devoid of human beings the world would thus have no meaning.

When the question of contraception comes up, many are hesitant, for that implies controlling the birth of human beings and hence tampering with the natural process of procreation. In order to dispel some of the misconceptions in this regard, we have seen that where pregnancy may injure the health of the woman or may even threaten her life, the higher purpose of protecting life, operating under the rubric known as the "the rule of necessity," would prevail, requiring a woman to make use of contraceptive devices to protect her health or life. The use of contraceptive devices for other reasons by mutual consent between the husband and wife is *makruh* (undesirable, improper), as Imam al Ghazali pointed out, but not necessarily *haram* (forbidden) under the *Shari'ah*.

The Qur'an defends the sanctity of life in the following words:

> If anyone slays a human being unless it be (in punishment) for murder or for spreading corruption on earth – it shall be as if he had slain the whole of mankind; whereas, if anyone saves a life, it shall be as if he had saved the lives of the whole of mankind (5:32).

From this verse it is evident that every human being has the right to be born, the right to be, and the right to live as long as Allah (SWT) permits. No one may be deprived of life except for a legitimate crime as discussed above. The fetus is regarded by all schools of Islamic law as having the right to life, as indicated by the fact that the death sentence on a pregnant woman can be carried out only after she has given birth.

The problem of pregnancy as a result of rape, cannot be solved by abortion. The only real solution is to curtail the free intermingling of sexes and impose strict punishments for those involved in such a crime. Moreover, after a lapse of time, it might not be readily ascertainable whether rape had indeed taken place. Hence, arbitrarily to sanction abortion for any pregnancy that is said to have resulted from rape might lead to abuse of such permission.

Even fear of fetal deformity is no excuse for abortion, because the extent of the deformity cannot be positively ascertained. Moreover, the very techniques that have enabled doctors to detect fetal deformity may in the near future be capable of curing or treating certain types of fetal deformity. The Islamic approach would be to focus on preventing the birth of defective infants, in the event that such is feared, by employing contraceptive measures rather than by resorting to abortion after fertilization and implantation have already taken place. Deeper research is needed in all three of the major issues addressed in this book.

APPENDIX SOURCES

" Hippocratic Oath and the Geneva Declaration" have been taken from: Beauchamp, Tom L. and Childress, J. F., *Principles of Biomedical Ethics* (New York: Oxford University Press, 1979), pp. 280-282.

"Oath of the Muslim Physician" has been taken from:
The International Organization of Islamic Medicine: Islamic Code of Medical Ethics (Kuwait Document: International Conference on Islamic Medicine, January 1981), p. 93.

APPENDIX 1
THE HIPPOCRATIC OATH

I swear by Apollo Physician and Asclepius and Hygieia and Panaceia and all the gods and goddesses, making them my witnesses, that I will fulfil according to my ability and judgment this oath and this covenant:

To hold him who has taught me this art as equal to my parents and to live my life in partnership with him, and if he is in need of money to give him a share of mine, and to regard his offspring as equal to my brothers in male lineage and to teach them this art - if they desire to learn it - without fee and covenant; to give a share of precepts and oral instruction and all the other learning to my sons and to the sons of him who has instructed me and to pupils who have signed the covenant and have taken an oath according to the medical law, but to no one else.

I will apply dietetic measures for the benefit of the sick according to my ability and judgment; I will keep them from harm and injustice.

I will neither give a deadly drug to anybody if asked for it, nor will I make a suggestion to this effect. Similarly I will not give to a woman an abortive remedy. In purity and holiness I will guard my life and my art.

I will not use the knife, not even on sufferers from stone, but will withdraw in favor of such men as are engaged in this work.

Whatever houses I may visit, I will come for the benefit of the sick, remaining free of all intentional injustice, of all mischief and in particular of sexual relations with both female and male persons, be they free or slaves.

What I may see or hear in the course of the treatment or even outside of the treatment in regard to the life of men, which on no account one must spread abroad, I will keep to myself holding such things shameful to be spoken about.

If I fulfil this oath and do not violate it, may it be granted to me to enjoy life and art, being honored with fame among all men for all time to come; if I transgress it and swear falsely, may the opposite of all this be my lot.

APPENDIX 2

THE WORLD MEDICAL ASSOCIATION DECLARATION OF GENEVA

Physician's Oath

At the time of being admitted as a member of the medical profession:

I solemnly pledge myself to consecrate my life to the service of humanity;

I will give to my teachers the respect and gratitude which is their due;

I will practice my profession with conscience and dignity: the health of my patient will be my first consideration;

I will maintain by all the means in my power, the honor and the traditions of the medical profession; my colleagues will be my brothers;

I will not permit considerations of religion, nationality, race, party politics, or social standing to intervene between my duty and my patient;

I will maintain the utmost respect for human life from the time of conception; even under threat, I will not use my medical knowledge contrary to the laws of humanity;

I make these promises solemnly, freely, and upon my honor.

APPENDIX 3

THE OATH OF THE MUSLIM DOCTOR

In the name of God, Most Gracious, Most Merciful.

I swear by God – the Great

To regard God in carrying out my profession.

To protect human life in all stages and under all circumstances, doing my utmost to rescue it from death, malady, pain, and anxiety:

To keep peoples' dignity, cover their privacies, and lock up their secrets–

To be, all the way, an instrument of God's mercy, extending my medical care to near and far, virtuous and sinner, and friend and enemy–

To strive in the pursuit of knowledge and to harness it for the benefit but not the harm of mankind–

To revere my teacher, teach my junior, and be a brother to members of the Medical Profession joined in piety and charity.

To live my Faith in private and in public, avoiding whatever blemishes me in the eyes of God, His Apostle, and my fellow Faithful.

And may God be witness to this Oath.

NOTES

INDRODUCTION

1. Isma'il Raji'al Faruqi, *Tawhid: Its Implications for Thought and Life,* (Wyncote PA: International Institute of Islamic Thought, 1982) p.73.
2. *Ibid.*, 66.
3. See Shwikar Ibrahim Elwan, "Constitutional Democracy in Islam," Ph.D. Diss., (Emory University, U.S.A., 1971), 44.
4. al Bukhari, Muhammad bin Isma'il: *Sahih al Bukhari* (Cairo: Dar al Sha'b, n.d.), "Kitab al Jumu'ah," p. 6.
5. al Darami, Abu Muhammad 'Abd al Rahman: *Sunan al Darami* (Cairo: Dar al Mahasin li al Tiba'ah, 1966), "Kitab al Nikah," vol. 2, Hadith no. 2175, p.58.
6. Ibn Majah, Abu 'Abd Allah bin Yazid: *Sunan Ibn Majah* (Cairo: Dar Ihya al Kutub al 'Arabiyyah, n.d.), "Al Muqaddimah," part 1, Hadith no. 224, p. 81.
7. Muslim ibn al Hajjaj al Naysaburi, *Sahih Muslim* (Cairo: Dar al Sha'b, n.d.), "Kitab al Salam," Hadith no. 68, Vol. 5, p. 51.
8. Ziauddin Sardar,: "Islamic Science or Science in Islamic Polity: What is the Difference?" in *Journal of Islamic Science* (Aligarh: The Muslim Association for the Advancement of Science, January 1985), vol. 1, no. 1, p. 42.

CHAPTER 1

1. Muslim ibn al Hajjaj al Naysaburi, *Sahih Muslim*, "Kitab al Qadr" (Cairo: Dar al Sha'b,n.d), 5:520-1.
2. *Sahih Muslim*, op. cit., "Kitab al Birr," Hadith no.66, Vol.4 pp.1999-2000.
3. Shams al Din Muhammad bin Abu Bakr bin Ayyub Ibn Qayyim al Jawziyyah: *al Tibb al Nabawi* (Beirut: al Maktabah al Thaqafiyyah, n.d.),2-3.
4. Ibn Sina (Avicenna), Abu Ali al Husayn Ibn Ali: *Kitab al Qanun fi al Tibb* (Cairo: Mu'assasah al Halabi wa Shurakahu li al Nashr wa al Tawzi' n.d.),1:3
5. *Musnad al Imam Ahmad bin Hanbal* (Beirut: Dar al Sadir li al Tiba'an wa al Nashr, n.d.),6:167.
6. Hossein Nasr, *Science and Civilization in Islam* (Pakistan: Suhail Academy, 1968),192-3.
7. Abu Dawud Sulayman ibn al As'ab Al Sijistani, *Sunan Abu Dawud*, "Kitab al Tibb" (Beirut: Dar Ihya al Sunnah al Nabawiyyah, n.d.),4:3.
8. *Sahih al Bukhari*, "Kitab al Tibb" (Cairo: Dar al Sha'b,n.d.), vol 3, pt.7:158.

9. Abu Dawud, *Sunan*, "Kitab al Diyah," 4:195.
10. Abu 'Abd Allah Ibn Majah, *Sunan*, "Kitab al Tibb" (Cairo: Dar al Kutub al 'Arabiyyah,n.d.), 2:1156,no.3493
11. M.M.Sharif, *A History of Muslim Philosophy* (Kempten, Germany: Allgauer Heimatverlag,1966),2:1334.
12. Ahmad Ibn Hanbal, *Musnad*, 1:192.
13. Abu 'Abd Allah Ibn Majah, *Sunan*, "Kitab al Tibb," 2:1142.
14. Shams al Din ibn Qayyim al Jawziyyah, *Al Tibb*,2.
15. Abu Dawud, *Sunan*, "Kitab al Tibb," 4:7
16. *Sahih al Bukhari*, "Kitab al Ashribah," 3,7:143.
17. *Sahih Muslim*, "Kitab al Ashribah," 5:166.
18. Aydin Sayili, "The Emergence of the Prototype of the Modern Hospital," *Studies in History and Medicine* (Tughlaqabad, New Delhi: Department of History of Medicine and Medical Research, June, 1980), vol.4, no. 2:113.

CHAPTER 2

1. Ahmad Elkadi, "Professional Ethics," *The Journal of the Islamic Medical Association Indianapolis*, Indiana, Sept. 1976,27.
2. Tom L. Beauchamp, and J.F. Childress, *Principles of Biomedical Ethics* (New York: Oxford University Press, 1979), 99.
3. *Ibid.*, 135.
4. *Ibid.*, 213.
5. *Ibid.*, 282.
6. See appendix below.
7. Abdul Hamid, "Medical Ethics in Islam," in *Studies in History and Medicine*, op. cit. chapter 1, note 18, vol.5, no. 2: 135.
8. *Sunan Abu Dawud*, op. cit., "Kitab al Manasik," part 2, p.185.
9. From Nizami-i-Arudi, *Chahar Maqala*, E.G. Browne trans., E.J.W. Gibb Memorial Series (London: Luzac and Co., 1921), vol. xi, 2, p.76.
10. Abu 'Abd Allah ibn Majah, *Sunan*, op. cit., *al Muqaddimah*, part 1:81, Hadith no. 224.
11. Abu 'Ali Ibn Sina, op. cit., vol.1, p.149.
12. David Suzuki, "Life at All Cost Is Too High a Price," *Reader's Digest* (South Africa: Reader's Digest Association (Pty) Ltd., November, 1985), 111-2.
13. Ahmad Elkadi, "Islamic Code," *The Journal of Islamic Medical Association*, op. cit., vol. 13, July 1981, p. 110.
14. Ibn Rushd, Abu Walid Muhammad bin Ahmad bin Muhammad bin Ahmad (Averroes), *Bidayah al Mujtahid*, 5th edition (Egypt: Matba'ah Mustafa al Babi al Halabi wa Awladuh, 1981, 2:418.
15. *Bulletin of Islamic Medicine*, 2nd ed. (Kuwait: Ministry of Public Health, January 1981) p.731.

CHAPTER 3

1. *Sahih al Bukhari*, op. cit.,"Kitab al Nikah," Part 7, p. 2.
2. *Ibid.*, Part 7, p. 3.
3. Isma'il Raji al Faruqi, *Islam*, (Texas: Argus Communications, 1979) p. 46.
4. Abul 'Ala Mawdudi, *Birth Control* (Lahore: Islamic Publications Ltd., 1976), p. 83.
5. Muhammad Saleem, *"Ethical Justification of Family Planning,"* *Islamic Studies Journal* (Pakistan: Islamic Research Institute) 8, no.3 (September 1969):257.

CHAPTER4

1. Mawdudi, *Birth Control*, op. cit., page 44, 180-181.
2. Abdel R. Omran, Islam and Fertility Control, *Egypt: Population Problems and Prospects* (North Carolina: Carolina Population Centre, University of N. Carolina, 1973), 172.
3. Abu Bakr Ahmad bin Ali al Razi Al Jassas: *Ahkam al Qur'an* (Beirut: Dar al Kitab al Arabi, 1335 A.H.), pt. 1:535.
4. Edward William Lane, *Arabic-English Lexicon* (New York: Frederick Ungar Publishing Co., 1956), Bk 1, pt 5:2036.
5. Akhter Hameed Khan, *"Islamic Opinion on Contraception,"* in *Muslim Attitudes toward Family Planning*, ed. Olivia Schieffelin (New York: The Population Council, 1973), 62.
6. Muhammad bin Ali bin Muhammad al Shawkani, *Nayl al Awtar* (Cairo: Maktabah Dar al Turath, n.d.), pt 5:195-6.
7. Ahmad Ali bin Hajar al Asqalani, *Fath al Bari* (Riyadh: al Maktabah al Salafiyyah, n.d.), pt 9:309.
8. Abu Hamid Muhammad al Ghazali, *Ihya ul ulum,* (Cairo: al Matba'ah al Azhariyyah al Misriyyah, 1302 A.H.), 2:52.
9. Ibn Qayyim al-Jawziyyah, *Zad al Ma'ad* (Egypt: Matba'ah Mustafa al Babi al Halabi wa Awladuhu, 1960), pt 4:21.
10. Abu Hamid Al Ghazali, *Ihya ul Ulum*, 2:51.
11. Ala al Din Ibn Mas'ud al Kasani, *Bada'i al Sana'i* (Cairo, A.H. 1322), 2:334.
12. Malik bin Anas, *Al Muwatta*, "Kitab al Nikah," 1st ed., (Beirut: Dar al Nafa'is, 1971), 409.
13. Abu Zakariyya Yahya bin Sharaf al Nawawi, *Commentary on Sahih Muslim*: Bab Hukm al 'Azl, vol. 3, p. 612.
14. Abu Muhammad Abd Allah bin Ahmad bin Muhammad Ibn Qudamah, *Al Mughni* (Cairo: Maktabah al Jumhuriyyah al Arabiyyah, n.d.), 7:23-4.
15. B.F. Musallam, *Sex and Society in Islam* (Cambridge: Cambridge University Press, 1983), 32.
16. *Sahih Bukhari*, op. cit., page 26 supra, "Kitab al Nikah," vol.3, pt 7:4.

17. al Ghazali, *Ihya ul Ulum*, 2:52.
18. Ahmad al Sharabassi, "*Islam and Family Planning*," in *Muslim Attitudes toward Family Planning*, ed. Olivia Schieffelin, New York: The Population Council, 1973), 110-11.

CHAPTER 5

1. Taqi al Din Ahmad Ibn Taymiyyah, *Al Fatawa al Kubra* (Cairo: Matba'ah Kurdistan al 'Ilmiyyah, A.H. 1326), 1:60, no. 36.
2. Zain al Abidin Ibn Ibrahim Ibn Nujaym, *Al Bahr al Ra'iq*, printed on the margin of al Marghinani's *Hidayah*, 3:215.
3. *South African Family Medical Adviser* (Cape Town: The Reader's Digest Association of South Africa (Pty) Ltd., 1983), 254.
4. Al Ghazali, *Ihya ul Ulum*, op. cit., 2:51.
5. See Ronald Munson, *Intervention and Reflection*, 2nd edit. (California: Wadsworth Publishing Co., 1983), 446.
6. Robert H. Glass, *Getting Pregnant in the 1980's* (Berkeley: University of California Press, 1982), 81.
7. Clive Wood, *Contraception Explained* (Geneva: World Health Organization, 1975), 45.
8. Muhammad Sa'id Ramadan al Buti, *Tahdid al Nasl* (Damascus: Maktabah al Farabi,1976), 33.
9. Muhammad 'Ali Al Sabuni, *Mukhtasar Tafsir Ibn Kathir*, 7th edition (Beirut: Dar al Qur'an, 1981), 2:603.
10. Abu Zakariyya Yahya bin Sharaf Al Nawawi, *Mughni al Muhtaj* (Egypt: Matba'ah Mustafa al Babi al Halabi wa Awladuhu, 1958), pt 3:126.
11. Mohammad al Bukhari, *Sahih*, op. cit., "Kitab al Nikah," Part 7, p.5.
12. Muslim, *Sahih*, op cit, "Kitab al Nikah," 3:553-4.
13. Clive Wood, *Vasectomy and Sterilization* (London: Maurice Temple Smith Ltd., 1974), 52.
14. Tahir Mahmood, *Family Planning: The Muslim Viewpoint* (New Delhi: Vikas Publishing House Prt. Ltd., 1977), 96.
15. *Ibid*, 98.
16. Ibn Hajar, *Fath al Bari*, 9:310.
17. Norman E. Himes, *Medical History of Contraception* (New York: Schocken Books Inc., 1970), 142,144-5,151,155.
18. B.F. Musallam, *Sex and Society in Islam* (Cambridge: Cambridge University Press, 1963), 62.
19. Muhammad Asad, *The Message of the Qur'an* (Gibraltar: Dar al Andalus Ltd., 1980), 128.
20. Ali Ibn Abbas, *Kamil al Sina'ah al Tibbiyyah* (Bulaq, Cairo, A.H. 1294), 2:439-40. Also see Musallam, B.F., op. cit., p. 70.
21. Abu Ali Ibn Sina, *Kitab al Qanun fi al Tibb*, op. cit., pt. 2:579. Also see Musallam, B.F., op. cit., p. 69.

CHAPTER 6

1. Musallam, B.F., *Sex*, op. cit., vii.
2. D.M. Feldman, *Birth Control in Jewish Law*, (New York: University Press 1968), chapter 13, *An Oral Contraceptive*, pp. 244-247.
3. Norman Anderson, *Issues of Life and Death* (London: Hodder and Stoughton, 1976), 63-4, and Musallam, op. cit., 27.
4. Joseph Fletcher, *Morals and Medicine* (Boston: Boston Press, 1954), 69.
5. Mawdudi, *Birth Control*, op. cit., pp. 8-9, 12-15.
6. Dudley Kirk, Factors Affecting Moslem Natality in Bernard Berelson, et al, eds., *Family Planning and Population Programs* (The University of Chicago Press, 1966) chapter 46, 561-79.
7. Mahmood Tahir, *Family Planning*, op. cit., p. 67.
8. Ministry of Health, Labour, and Social Welfare, Government of Pakistan, *Family Planning Schemes for Pakistan during the Third Five-Year Plan Period, 1965-70*, p.148.
9. Khalifa Abdul Hakim, "*Islam and Birth Control*", in Maulana Shah Muhammad Jafar Nadvi Phulvarvi, *Birth Control* (Lahore: Pakistan, June 1959).
10. Muhammad Shahidullah, "Family Planning and Islam", paper presented to the First Indian Ocean Conference, International Planned Parenthood Federation, Dacca, East Pakistan, January 1962.
11. Fazlur Rahman, "Religion and Planned Parenthood in Pakistan", paper presented at the Seminar on Population, Karachi, March 1964.
12. Mawdudi, *Birth Control*, op. cit., 136.
13. See Fazlur Rahman, op. cit.

CHAPTER 7

1. Paul D. Simmons, *Birth and Death Bioethical Decision-Making* (Philadelphia: The Westminster Press, 1983), 157.
2. *Sunan al Nasa'i*, "Kitab al Nikah," (Beirut: Dar al Turath Al Arabi, n.d.), pt.6:66.
3. Muhammad Ali al Sabuni, *Tafsir Ibn Kathir*, op. cit., 3:282-3.
4. M.F.R. Ansari, *Qur'anic Foundations and Structure of Muslim Society*, Ist ed., (Karachi: Trade and Industry Publications Ltd., 973), 2:196.
5. Hammudah Abdalati, *Islam in Focus* (Maryland: International Graphics Printing Service, 1975), 172.
6. Sufi Muhammad Azizur Rehman Sahib Panipati, *Aina-e-Amaliyat* (Delhi: Dini Book Depot, n.d.), 19.
7. *Tafsir Ibn Kathir*, op. cit.,3:81.
8. Hammudah Abdalati, *Islam in Focus*, op. cit., 171.

CHAPTER 8

1. R. Leibowitz, "The Facts of Infertility", *Living & Loving*, (Durban: Republican Press (Pty) Ltd). October 1985, no 197, p. 41.

2. Robert H. Glass and Ronald J. Ericsson, *Getting Pregnant in the 1980s*, (California: University of California Press, 1982), 41-2, 47.
3. *Ibid.*, 12, 20, 29.
4. Paul D. Simons, op. cit., 160-3.

CHAPTER 9
1. Sania Hamady, *Temperament and Character of the Arabs*, (New York: Twayne Publishers, 1959), 186.
2. Muslim, *Sahih*, "Kitab al Salam," op. cit., 15:51, Hadith no.68.
3. Haidar Bammate, *Muslim Contribution to Civilization* (Takoma Park, Md. Crescent Publications, n.d.), 29-32.
4. Ronald Munson, *Intervention and Reflection*, 2d. ed. (Belmont: Wadsworth Publishing Company, 1983), 433.
5. Ibid.
6. Glass and Ericsson, *Getting Pregnant*, op. cit., 39.
7. "Test-Tube babies not the Answer" in *The Daily News*, Durban, November 22, 1982.
8. Muslim, *Sahih*, "Kitab al Nikah," op. cit., 3:546, Hadith no. 1.
9. Abd al Rahman al Juzayri, *Kitab al Fiqh 'ala al Madhahib al Arba'ah* (Beirut: Dar al Fikr al Arabi, n.d.), 5:137.
10. Musallam, *Sex*, op. cit., 34.
11. Abd al Rahman al Juzayri, op.cit., 5:137.
12. Sa'id Ramadan, *Islamic Law: Its Scope and Equity*, 2d.ed.(Geneva: Publisher Unknown, 1970), 71.
13. Munson, *Intervention*, op. cit., 442.
14. Mahmud Shaltut, *al Fatawa* (Cairo: Matbu'at al Idarat al 'Ammat lil Thaqafah of al Azhar, December 1959), 300.
15. Yusuf al Qaradawi: *The Lawful and the Prohibited in Islam* (Arabic original, *Al Halal Wa al Haram fi al Islam*, 1960) (Indianapolis: American Trust Publications, n.d.), 227.
16. Qur'an 2:234.
17. Thomas J. O'Donnell, *Medicine and Christian Morality*, (New York: Alba House, 1976), 265.
8. Joseph F. Fletcher, *Morals and Medicine*, (Boston: Boston Press, 1954), 122.
19. Immanuel Jakobovits, *Jewish Medical Ethics*, (New York: Bloch Publishing Co., 1967), 248.
20. O'Donnell, *Medicine*, op. cit., 266.
21. "Children's Right to Legitimacy," *The Daily News*, Durban, September 12, 1984.
22. Munson, *Intervention*, op. cit., 435.
23. Ibid., 435-6.
24. Simmons, *Birth*, op. cit., page 90 supra, 160.
25. Paul Ramsey, *Shall We Produce*, Journal of the American Medical Association, (June 12, 1972):1481.

26. Abu Hamid al Ghazali, *Ihya ul Ulum*, op. cit.,page.58 supra, 2:51.
27. James B. Nelson, *Human Medicine*, (Minneapolis: Augsburg Publishing House, 1973),97.
28. Haring Bernard, *Medical Ethics* (St Paul Publication,1972) p.94.
29. Simmons, *Birth*, op. cit., page 90 supra, 176.
30. *Womb Leasing Causes Row*, The Natal Mercury, May 23, 1984.
31. Yusuf al Qaradawi, *The Lawful and the Prohibited in Islam*, op.cit, 179.
32. Charles Hamilton, *The Hedaya* (Lahore: Premier Book House, 1963), 619.
33. Al-Haj Muhammad Fazlul Karim, op. cit., vol. II, 72.
34. "One Pregnancy – Two Mothers," *Loving & Living*, July 1987, No. 218, pp. 18-21.

CHAPTER 10
1. Simmons, *Birth*, op. cit., 67.
2. Munson, *Intervention*, op. cit., 44.
3. Muhammad Asad, *The Message of the Qur'an*, (Gibralter: Dar al Andalus, 1980), 423, n.38.
4. Abdullah Yusuf Ali, *The Holy Qur'an: Text, Translation and Commentary* (Lahore: Sh. Muhammad Ashraf, Kashmiri Bazar, 1969), 703, n.2214, and 1694, n.5977.
5. *Mukhtasar Tafsir Ibn Kathir*, op. cit., vol.l, p.379.
6. M.H.K. Sherwani, *Hadrat Abu Bakr the First Caliph of Islam*, trans. by S.M.Haq (Lahore: Sh. Muhammad Ashraf, 1959), 60-61.
7. M.M. Azami, *Studies in Hadith Methodology and Literature*, (Indianapolis: American Trust Publications, 1977), 7.
8. Muhammad Qutb, *Islam the Misunderstood Religion* (Stuttgart: Ernst Klett Printers, 1977), 135.
9. Mian Rashid Ahmad Khan, *Islamic Jurisprudence* (Lahore: Sh. Muhammad Ashraf, 1978), 50.
10. A.F. Bahnasi, *Madkhal al Fiqh al Jina'i al Islami*, 2nd ed. (Beirut: Dar al Shuruq, 1980), 51-52.
11. Muslim, 4:265-66, *Sahih*, op. cit., "Kitab al Hudud."
12. Abd al Qadir 'Awdah, *Al Tashri' al Jina'i al Islami Muqaranah bi al Qanun al Wad'i* (Cairo: Dar al Turath, Matba'ah al Madani, n.d.), 2:384.
13. Bahnasi, *Madkhal*, op. cit., 93.
14. S.A. Rahman, *Punishment of Apostasy in Islam* (Lahore: Institute of Islamic Culture, 1972), 9.
15. Al Haj Muhammad Fazlul Karim, *Al Hadis: An English Translation and Commentary of Mishkat al Masabih* (Lahore: The Book House, n.d.), 2:524, no. 74.
16. Bahnasi, *Madkhal*, op. cit., 97.
17. Abdullah Yusuf Ali, *The Holy Qur'an*, op. cit., 70, n 182.

CHAPTER 11

1. The Church Assembly Board for Social Responsibility, *Abortion: an Ethical Discussion* (Westminster: Church Information Office, Church House, 1968), 7.

2. D.Ch. Overdiun, "The Ethics of Abortion," in *New Perspectives on Human Abortion*, eds. T. W. Hilgers, et al (Maryland: University Publications of America Inc., 1981), 369.

3. Lane, *Arabic-English Lexicon*, op.cit., 1,2:463.

4. Munson, *Introduction*, op.cit., 41.

5. Abu Fadl Shihab al Din Sayyid Mahmud al Alusi, *Ruh al Ma'ani* (Beirut: Ihya al Turath al Arabi, n.d.), pt. 27:64.

6. Muhammad Al Buti, *Tahdid al Nasl*, op.cit., 197.

7. Muhammad Salam Madkur, *Al Janin wa al Ahkam al Muta Alliqah bihi fi al Fiqh al Islami* (Cairo: Dar al Nahdah al Arabiyyah, 1969), 32.

8. Simmons, *Birth*, op. cit., 79-80.

9. Muslim, *Sahih*, op.cit., "Kitab Al-Qadr," 5:496 10. Ibid, 499-500.

11. Maurice Bucaille, *What is the Origin of Man*, 9th ed. (Paris: Seghers, 1983), 183.

12. Muhammad Ali al Bar, "Embryological Data in the Holy Qur'an," in *Abstract of the Proceedings of the 8th Saudi Medical Conference* (Riyadh: National Guard Printing Press, King Khalid Military Academy, 1983), 263.

13. Maurice Bucaille, *What is the Origin of Man*, op. cit., 185.

14. Mohammad Al Bar, *Abstract*, op. cit., 264.

15. Madkur, *Al-Janin*, op. cit., 84.

16. Abu Ja'far Muhammad Jarir al Tabari, *Tafsir al Tabari* (Beirut: Dar al Ma'rifah, n.d.), 9:90.

17. Abu 'Abd Allah Muhammad Idris al Shafi'i, *al Umm* (Beirut: Dar al Ma'rifah li al Tiba'ah wa al Nashr, n.d.) 6,136. Muhammad Ibn Qudamah, *Al-Mughni*, op. cit., 7:731; and Shams al Din al Dasuqi, *Hashiyah al Dasuqi* (Cairo: Dar Ihya al Kutub al Arabiyyah, n.d.), 4:322.

18. Muhammad Ibn Qudamah, *Al-Mughni*,op.cit., 2:551.

19. Madkur, *al-Janin*, op. cit., 287-288.

20. Muhammad Amin Ibn Abidin, *Hashiyah Radd al Muhtar* (Beirut: Dar al Fikr, 1979), 2:228.

21. Ibid.

CHAPTER 12

1. Muhammad Fazlur Rahman Ansari, *Foundations of Faith* (Karachi: World Federation of Islamic Missions, 1974), 15.

2. *Sahih al Bukhari*, "Kitab al Nikah," op. cit., 3,7:3.

3. London Sunday Times Reporter, "Unwed Virtue out of Fashion" in *The Sunday Times*, Durban, South Africa, 6 May, 1984.

4. Simmons, *Birth*, op. cit., 66.

5. Muhammad Qutb, *Islam The Misunderstood Religion* (Stuttgart: Ernst Klett Printers, 1977), 136.
6. *Muslim*, "Kitab al Hudud," op. cit., 4:277-78.
7. Sandra Kathleen Mahkorn and William V. Dolan, "Sexual Assault and Pregnancy," in New Perspectives on Human Abortion, op. cit., p.182.
8. Jennifer Wild, "Rape, Abortion and our Inadequate Legal System," in *The Sunday Tribune*, Durban, November 13, 1983.
9. "Report Claims Men React to Porn and Violence," in *The Daily News*, Durban, August 30, 1984.
10. Mahkorn and Dolan, op. cit., 187.
11. Ibid., 185-186.
12. Abu Abd Allah Muhammad Ibn Ahmad al Ansari Al Qurtubi, *Al Jami fi Ahkam al Qur'an* (Cairo, 1967, reprint), 12:8.
13. Joseph Fletcher, *Humanhood: Essays in Biomedical Ethics* (Prometheus Books, 1979), 138.
14. Monteleone, Patricia L. and Moraczewski, Albert S: "Medical and Ethical Aspects of Prenatal Diagnosis of Genetic Disease," in *New Perspectives on Human Abortion*, op. cit., pp. 46-48.
15. Issued by Dar al Ifta', No. 2484, dated 16.7.1403 A.H.
16. Musa, A: "The Fetal Alcohol Syndrome" in *Bulletin of Islamic Medicine* (Kuwait: Ministry of Public Health January 1981) vol. 1, 2nd edition, p. 377.
17. *Qur'an*, 5:90.
18. "The Price of Promiscuity" in *Sunday Times Magazine*, Durban, May 12, 1985, p. 15.
19. *Qur'an,* 17:32.
20. Alfi. O.S: "Marry from afar to avoid weak progeny" in *Bulletin of Islamic Medicine*, op. cit., vol. 1, 2nd edition, p. 338.
21. Simpson, N.E., et al.: *Prenatal Diagnosis of Genetic Disease in Canada: Report of a Collaborative Study*, Canad. Med. Assoc. J. 115:739, 1976.
22. Refer Lane's *Arabic-English Lexicon*, op. cit., Bk 1, part 5, p. 1811.
23. *Sahih al Bukhari*, "Kitab al Nikah", op. cit., Part 7, vol. 3, p. 3.
24. Al Ghazali, op. cit., vol. 2, p. 51.
25. *Qur'an*, 64:15.
26. Monteleone and Moraczewski, op. cit., p. 52.
27. O'Donnell, Thomas J: *Medicine and Christian Morality* (New York: Alba House, 1976), pp. 186-7.
28. Ibid., p. 187.

CHAPTER 13

1. Mohammed Mekki Naciri, "A View of Family Planning in Islamic Legislation," in *Muslim Attitudes Toward Family Planning*, ed. Olivia Schieffelin (New York: The Population Council, 1973), 144.

2. Yusuf al Qardawi, *Al Halal wa al Haram fi al Islam*, 14th ed. (Cairo: Maktabah al Wahbah, 1980), 169.
3. Muhammad Ibn Abidin, *Hashiyah*, op. cit., 3:176.
4. Muhammad ibn 'Arafah Dasuqi, op. cit., 2:266-7.
5. al Ghazali, op. cit., 2:51.
6. Ibn Qudamah, *al-Mughni,* op. cit., 7:815-6.
7. Muhammad al Buti, *Tahdid al Nasl*, op. cit., 96-99.
8. Yusuf al Qaradawi, *The Lawful*, op. cit., 202.
9. Manfred Ullmann, *Islamic Medicine* (Edinburgh: Edinburgh University Press, 1978), 43.
10. Musallam, *Sex and Society in Islam*, op. cit., 71. For original document see al Razi, Abu Bakr: *Kitab al Hawi fi al Tibb* (Heyderabad: Osmania Oriental Publications Bureau, 1960) 9:139.
11. Ali Ibn al 'Abbas, *Kamil al Sina'ah al Tibbiyyah* (Cairo: Bulaq, 1294 A.H.), 2:439-40.
12. Manfred Ullmann, op. cit., 45.
13. Abu 'Ali Ibn Sina, *Kitab fi al Tibb*, 2:575.
14. Vernet J: "Ibn Hubal" in *The Encyclopadeia of Islam*, ed. B. Lewis et al (Leiden: E.J. Brill, 1971, new edition) vol. 3, p. 802.
15. Ibn Hubal, Abid al Hasan Ali ibn Ahmad ibn Ali: *Kitab al Mukhtarat fi al Tibb* (Heyderabad, A.H. 1364) vol. 4, p. 60.
16. Watson, "*Urologic Complications*," op. cit., 143.
17. Matthew, "*Complications*," op. cit., 147-148.
18. Hilgers, "*Abortion*" op. cit., 90.

Chapter 14
1. 'Abd al Qadir 'Awdah, *Al-Tashri'*, op. cit., 5.
2. Al Nawawi, *Mughni al-Muhtaj*, cit., 4:103.
3. Id.
4. Id.
5. Id.
6. Lane: *Arabic-English Lexicon*, op. cit., 1,6:2238.
7. Bukhari, *Sahih*, op. cit, 3,9:14.
8. Muhammad Al Buti, *Tahdid al Nasl*, op.cit., 200.
9. Abu Walid Ibn Rushd, *Bidayah*, op. cit., 2:416.
10.'Abd al Qadir 'Awdah, *Al-Tashri'*, op. cit., 295.
11. *Mawsu'ah Jamal Abd al Nasir fi al Fiqh al Islami* (Cairo: al Majlis al 'Ala li al Shu'un al Islamiyyah, 1388 A.H.), 3:161.
12. Ibn 'Abidin, *Hashiya*, op. cit., 6:588.
13. Al Bukhari, *Sahih*, op.cit., vol. 3, part 9, p.14.
14. *Sunan al Nasa'i* , op. cit., 8:47.
15. Abu Dawud, *Sunan*, op. cit., "Kitab al Diyah," 4:193.
16. Sayyid Sabiq, *Fiqh al Sunnah*, 5th ed. (Kuwait:Dar al Bayan, 1971), 2:478.

17. Ibn Abidin, *Hashiya*, op. cit., 6:589.
18. Muhammad al Buti, op. cit., 201.
19. Abu Muhammad Ibn Qudamah, *Al-Mughni*, op.cit., 7:806.
20. Abu Walid Ibn Rushd, *Bidayah*, op. cit., 2:415.
21. Ibid. 416.
22. Abu Zakariyya al Nawawi, *Mughni al Muhtaj*, op.cit., 4:103.
23. Abu Muhammd Ibn Qudamah, *Al-Mighni*, op. cit., 7:816.
24. Muhammad al Buti, op. cit., 205.
25. Abu Muhammad Ibn Qudamah, *Al-Mughni*, op. cit., 7:812.
26.'Abd al Qadir 'Awdah, *Al Tashri'*, op.cit., 298.
27. Sayyid Sabiq, *Fiqh al Sunnah*, op. cit., 2:466-7.
28. J. Milton Cowan, ed., Hans Wehr, *A Dictionary of Modern written Arabic* (London: George Allen and Unwin Ltd., 1971), 833.
29. *Qur'an*, 4:92, also states: If one does not find (the wealth with which to free) a slave then one has to fast for two months consecutively.
30. Abu Walid Ibn Rushd, op. cit., 2:416; and Abu Muhammad Ibn Qudamah, *Al Mighni*, op. cit., 7:816.
31. Ibn Abidin, *Hashiya*, op. cit., 6:590.
32. Abu Walid Ibn Rushd, *Bidayah*, op. cit., 2:417.
33. Abu Bakr Ahmad bin Ali al Razi Al Jassas, op. cit., 2:246.
34. 'Abd al Qadir 'Awdah, *Al Tashri'*, op. cit., 302.
35. Abu Walid Ibn Rushd, *Bidayah*, op. cit., 2:418.

CONCLUSION

1. Isma'il al Faruqi, *Tawhid*, op. cit., 77.

SOURCES

A. ARABIC SOURCES

1. al Alusi, Abu Fadl Shihab al Din al Sayyid Mahmud, *Ruh al Ma'ani* (Beirut: Ihya al Turath al Arabi, n.d.), 15 vols.

2. 'Awdah, 'A., *Al Tashri' al Jina'i al Islami Muqaranah bi al Qanun al Wada'i* (Cairo: Dar al Turath, Matba'ah al Madani, n.d.), 2 vols.

3. Bahnasi, A.F. *Madkhal fi al Fiqh al Jina'i al Islami* (Beirut: Dar al Shuruq, 2nd Edition, 1980).

4. al Bukhari, Muhammad ibn Isma'il, *Sahih al Bukhari* (Cairo: Dar al Sha'b, n.d.), 3 vols.

5. al Buti, Muhammad Sa'id Ramadan. *Tahdid al Nasl* (Damascus: Maktabah al Farabi, 1976).

6. Dar al Ifta. *Fatwa no. 2484* (Dar al Ifta: Riyadh, 16-7-1403).

7. al Dasuqi, Shams al Din Muhammad Ibn 'Arafah. *Hashiyah al Dasuqi* (Cairo: Dar Ihya al Kutub al 'Arabiyyah, n.d.), 4 vols.

8. al Ghazali, Abu Hamid Muhammad bin Muhammad. *Ihya ul 'Ulum al Din* (Cairo: Matba'ah al Istiqamah, n.d.), 4 vols.

9. Ibn al 'Abbas, 'Ali, *Kamil al Sina'ah al Tibbiyyah* (Bulaq, Cairo, 1294 A.H.)

10. Ibn 'Abidin, Muhammad Amin Ibn Umar, *Hashiyah Radd al Muhtar* (Beirut: Dar al Fikr, 1979), 8 vols.

11. Ibn Anas, Malik. *Al Muwatta* (Beirut: Dar al Nafa'is, 1971).

12. Ibn Hajar al 'Asqalani, Ahmad Ibn 'Ali, *Fath al Bari* (Riyadh: al Maktabah al Salafiyyah, n.d.), 13 vols.

13. Ibn Hanbal, Ahmad, *Musnad al Imam Ibn Hanbal* (Beirut: Dar al Sadir li al Tiba'ah wa al Nashr, n.d.), 6 vols.

14. Ibn Hubal, 'Abid al Hassan 'Ali Ibn Ahmad Ibn 'Ali, *Kitab al Mukhtarat fi al Tibb* (Haydarabad, A.H.1364).

15. Ibn Majah, Abu 'Abd Allah Muhammad bin Yazid, *Sunan Ibn Majah* Cairo: Dar Ihya al kutub al 'Arabiyyah, n.d.), 2 vols.

16. Ibn Nujaym, Zain al 'Abidin Ibn Ibrahim, *Al Bahr al Ra'iq* (printed on the margin of al Marghinani's Hidayah).

17. Ibn Qudamah, Muhammad 'Abd Allah bin Ahmad bin Muhammad, *Al Mughni* (Riyadh: Maktabah al Riyadh al Hadithah, n.d.), 9 vols.

18. Ibn Rushd, Abu Walid Muhammad bin Ahmad bin Muhammad, *Bidayah al Mujtahid* (Egypt: Matba'ah Mustafa al Babi al Halabi wa Awladuh, 1981, 5th Edition), 2 vols.

19. Ibn Sina, Abu 'Ali al Husayn, *Kitab al Qanun fi al Tibb* (Cairo: Mu'assasah al Halabi wa Shurakahu li al Nashr wa al Tawzi', n.d.), 3 vols.

20. Ibn Taymiyyah, Taqi al Din Ahmad, *Al Fatawa al Kubra* (Cairo:

Matba'ah Kurdistan al 'Ilmiyyah, 1326 A.H.), 5 vols.
21. al Jassas, Abu Bakr Ahmad bin 'Ali al Razi, *Ahkam al Qur'an* (Beirut: Dar al kutub al Arabi, n.d.), 3 vols.
22. al Juzayri, 'Abd al Rahman, *Kitab al Fiqh 'ala al Madhahib al Arba'ah* (Beirut: Dar al Fikr al 'Arabi, n.d.), 5 vols.
23. al Jawziyyah, Ibn Qayyim Shams al Din Abu 'Abd Allah Muhammad ibn Abu Bakr, *Zad al Ma'ad* (Egypt: Matba ah Mustafa al Babi al Halabi wa Awladuh, 1960), 2 vols.
24. *Al Tibb al Nabawi* (Beirut: al Maktabah al Thaqafiyyah, n.d.).
25. al Kasani, 'Ala al Din Ibn Mas'ud, *Bada'i al Sana'i* (Cairo, 322 A.H.).
26. Madkur, Muhammad Salam, *Al Janin al Ahkam al Muta'alliqah bihi fi al Fiqh al Islami* (Cairo: Dar al Nahdah al 'Arabiyyah, 1969).
27. *Mawsu'ah Jamal 'Abd al Nasir fi al Fiqh al Islami* (Cairo: Majlis al 'Ala li al Shu'un al Islamiyyah, 1388 A.H.), Part 3.
28. Naysaburi, Muslim ibn al Hajjaj, *Sahih Muslim* (Cairo: Dar al Sha'b, n.d.), 5 vols.
29. al Nawawi, Abu Zakariyya Yahya bin Sharaf, *Mughni al Muhtaj* (Egypt: Matba'ah Mustafa al Babi al Halabi wa Awladuh, 1908), 4 vols.
30. al Qaradawi, Yusuf. *Al Halal wa al Haram fi al Islam* (Cairo: Maktabah al Wahbah, 1980, 14th Edition).
32. al Qurtubi, Abu 'Abd Allah Muhammad Ibn Ahmad al Ansari, *Al Jami' li ahkam al Qur'an* (Cairo, 1967, reprint).
33. al Razi, Abu Bakr, *Kitab al Hawi fi al Tibb* (Heyderabad: Osmania Oriental Publications Bureau, 1960).
34. Sabiq, Sayyid, *Fiqh al Sunnah* (Kuwait: Dar al Bayan, 1971), 3 vols.
35. al Sabuni, Muhammad 'Ali, *Muktasar Tafsir Ibn Kathir* (Beirut: Dar al Qur'an al Karim, 7th Edition, 1981), 3 vols.
36. al Shafi'i, Abu 'Abd Allah Muhammad Idris, *Kitab al Umm* (Beirut: Dar al Ma'rifah li al Tiba'ah wa al Nashr, n.d.), 4 vols.
37. Shaltut, Mahmud, *Al Fatawa* (Cairo: Matba'at al Idarah al 'Ammah lil Thaqafah of al Azhar, December 1959).
38. al Shawkani, Muhammad bin 'Ali bin Muhammad, *Nayl al Awtar* (Cairo: Maktabah Dar al Turath, n.d.), 4 vols.
39. al Sijistani, Abu Dawud Sulayman ibn al As'ab, *Sunan Abu Dawud* (Beirut: Dar Ihya al Sunnah al Nabawiyyah, n.d.), 2 vols.
40. al Tabari, Abu Ja'far Muhammad Jarir, *Tafsir al Tabari* (Beirut: Dar al Ma'rifah, n.d.), 12 vols.

B. ENGLISH SOURCES

(i) BOOKS

1. Abdalati, Hammudah, *Islam in Focus* (Maryland: International Graphics Printing Service, 1975).

2. Ali, Abdullah Yusuf, *The Holy Qur'an: Text Translation and Commentary* (Lahore: Sh. Muhammad Ashraf. Kashmiri Bazar 1969).
3. Ansari, Maulana Muhammad Fazl-ur-Rahman, *Foundations of Faith* (Karachi: World Federation of Islamic Missions, 1974).
4. *The Qur'anic Foundations and Structure of Muslim Society* (Karachi, Pakistan: Trade and Industry Publications Ltd.), 1973. 2 vols.
5. Asad, Muhammad, *The Message of the Qur'an* (Gibraltar: Dar al Andalus, 1980).
6. Azami, M.M. *Studies in Hadith Methodology and Literature* (Indianapolis: American Trust Publications, 1977).
7. Bammate, Haidar, *Muslim Contribution to Civilization* (Takoma Park Md: The Crescent Publications, n.d.).
8. Beauchamp, Tom L. and Childress, J.F., *Principles of Biomedical Ethics* (New York: Oxford University Press, 1979).
9. Bucaille, M. *What is the Origin of Man?* (Paris: Seghers, 1983, 9th Edition).
10. The Church Assembly Board for Social Responsibility, *Abortion: An Ethical Discussion* (Westminster: Church Information Office, Church House, 1968).
11. Cowan, J. Milton, ed. Hans Wehr, *A Dictionary of Modern Written Arabic* (London: George Allen and Unwin Ltd., 1971).
12. Elwan, Shwikar Ibrahim, *Constitutional Democracy in Islam* (unpublished Ph.D. dissertation, Emory University, 1971).
13. Al Faruqi, Isma'il R. *Tawhid: Its Implications for Thought and Life* (Wyncote, Philadelphia: International Institute of Islamic Thought, 1982).
14. Fletcher, Joseph F. *Morals and Medicine* (Boston: Boston Press, 1954).
15. *Joseph Fletcher Humanhood: Essays in Biomedical Ethics* (Prometheus Books, 1979).
16. Glass, Robert H., *Getting Pregnant in the 1980s* (California: University of California Press, 1982).
17. Hamady, Sania, *Temperament and Character of the Arabs* (New York: Twayne Publishers, 1959).
18. Haneef, Suzane, *What everyone should know about Islam and Muslims* (Chicago: Kazi Publications, 1979).
19. Hanifi, M.A., *A Survey of Muslim Institutions and Culture* (Lahore: Ashraf Press, 1969).
20. Haring, Bernard, *Medical Ethics* (St. Pauls Publications, 1972).
21. Himes, Norman E., *Medical History of Contraception* (New York: Schocken Books Inc., 1970).
22. Jakobovits, Immanuel, *Jewish Medical Ethics* (New York: Bloch Publishing Company, 1967).
23. Karim, al Haj Muhammad Fazlul, *Al Hadis: An English Translation and Commentary of Mishkat al Masabih* (Lahore: The Book House, n.d.), 4 vols:

24. Khan, Mian Rashid Ahmad, *Islamic Jurisprudence* (Lahore: Sh. Muhammad Ashraf, Kashmiri Bazar, 1978).
25. Lane, Edward William, *Arabic-English Lexicon* (New York: Frederick Ungar Publishing Co., 1955).
26. Mahmood, Tahir, *Family Planning: The Muslim Viewpoint* (New Delhi: Vikas Publishing House, Pvt Ltd, 1977).
27. Mawdudi, A.A. *Birth Control* (Lahore: Islamic Publications Ltd., 1976).
28. Munson, Ronald, Intervention and Reflection, *Basic Issues in Medical Ethics* (California: Wadsworth Publishing Co., 2nd Edition, 1983).
29. Musallam, B.F. *Sex and Society in Islam* (Cambridge: Cambridge University Press, 1983).
30. Nasr, S.H. *Science and Civilization in Islam* (Pakistan: Suhail Academy, 1968).
31. Nelson, James B. *Human Medicine* (Minneapolis: Augsburg Publishing House, 1973).
32. O'Donnell, Thomas J., *Medicine and Christian Morality* (New York: Alba House, 1976).
33. Panipati, Sufi Muhammad Azizur Rahman, *Aina-e-Amaliyat* (Delhi: Dini Book Depot, n.d.).
34. Qutb Muhammad, *Islam the Misunderstood Religion* (W. Germany: Ernst Klett Printers, Stuttgart, 1977).
35. Rahman, Afzalur, *Qur'anic Sciences* (London: The Muslim Schools Trust, 1981).
36. Rahman, S.A. *Punishment of Apostasy in Islam* (Lahore: Institute of Islamic Culture, 1972).
37. Ramadan, Sa'id, *Islamic Law - Its Scope and Equity* (Geneva: publisher unknown, 2nd edition, 1970).
38. Sharif, M.M., *A History of Muslim Philosophy* (Kempten, Germany: Allgauer Heimatverag, 1966), 2 vols.
39. Sherwani, M.H.K. *Hadrat Abu Bakr the First Caliph of Islam* trans. by S.M. Haq (Lahore: Sh. Muhammad Ashraf, Kashmiri Bazar, 1959).
40. Simmons, Paul D., *Birth and Death: Bioethical Decision-making* (Philadelphia: The Westminster Press, 1983).
41. *South African Family Medical Adviser* (Cape Town: The Reader's Digest Association South Africa (Pty) Ltd., 1983).
42. Ullman, Manfred, *Islamic Medicine* (Edinburgh: Edinburgh University Press, 1978).
43. Wood, Clive, *Vasectomy and Sterilization* (London: Maurice Temple Smith Ltd., 1974).

(ii) ARTICLES
1. Abdul Hamid, "Medical Ethics in Islam" in *Studies in History and Medicine* (Tughlaqabad, New Delhi: Department of History and Medicine, June 1981).

2. Alfi, S.O., "Marry from Afar to Prevent Weak Progeny" in *Bulletin of Islamic Medicine* (Kuwait: Ministry of Public Health, 2nd Edition, January, 1981).
3. al Bar, Muhammad 'Ali, "Embryological Data in the Holy Qur'an" in *Abstract of the Proceedings of the 8th Saudi Medical Conference* (Riydh: National Guard Printing Press, King Khalid Military Academy, 1983).
4. Elkadi, Ahmed, "Professional Ethics" in *The Journal of the Islamic Medical Association* (Indianapolis: Indiana, September 1976).
5. "Islamic Code of Medical Professional Ethics" in *The Journal of Islamic Medical Association* (Indianapolis, Indiana, July 1981).
6. Hilgers, T.W., "Abortion Related Material Mortality: An In-Depth Analysis" in *New Perspectives on Human Abortion*, ed. T.W. Hilgers (Lanham, Maryland: University Press of America Inc., 1981).
7. Khan, Akhter Hameed, "Islamic Opinion on Contraceptive" in *Muslim Attitudes Toward Family Planning*, ed. Olivia Schieffelin (New York: The Population Council, 1973).
8. Leibowitz, R., "The Facts of Infertility" in *Living and Loving* (Durban: Republican Press (Pty) Ltd., October 1985, no. 197).
9. Mahkorn, Sandra Kathleen, and Dolan, William V., "Sexual Assault and Pregnancy" in *New Perspectives on Human Abortion*, ed. T.W. Hilgers, et al.(Lanham, Maryland : University Press of America Inc., 1981).
10. Mathew, J.B., "Complications of Legal Abortion: A Perspective from Private Practice" in *New Perspectives on Human Abortion*, ed. T.W. Hilgers, et al. (Lanham, Maryland: University Press of America Inc., 1981).
11. Monteleone, Patricia L., and Moraczewski, Albert S., "Medical and Ethical Aspects of Prenatal Diagnosis of Genegic Disease" in *New Perspectives on Human Abortion*, ed. T.W. Hilgers, et al. (Lanham, Maryland: University Press of America Inc., 1981).
12. Moosa, A., "The Fetal Alcohol Syndrome" in *Bulletin of Islamic Medicine* (Kuwait: Ministry of Public Health, 2nd Edition, January 1981).
13. Naciri, Mohammed Mekki. "A View of Family Planning in Islamic Legislation" in *Muslim Attitudes Toward Family Planning*, ed. Olivia Schieffelin (New York: The Population Council, 1973).
14. Nizami Arudi, *Chahar Mawala*, trans. by E.G. Browne (E.J.W. Gibb Memorial Series, vol. XI, 2, London: Luzac and Co., 1921).
15. Omran, Abdel R. "Islam and Fertility Control" in *Egypt: Population Problems and Prospects* (Carolina: Carolina Population Center, University of N. Carolina, 1973).
16. Overduim, D. Ch., "The Ethics of Abortion" in *New Perspectives on Human Abortion*, ed. T.W. Hilgers, et al. (Maryland: University Publications of America Inc., 1981).
17. Ramsey, Paul, "Shall We Reproduce?" II, *Journal of the American Medical Association*, June 12, 1972.
18. Saleem, M., "Ethical Justification of Family Planning" in *Islamic Studies Journal* (Pakistan: Islamic Research Institute, September 1969) vol.

VIII, No. 3.
19. Sardar, Ziauddin. "Islamic Science or Science in Islamic Polity: What Is the Difference?" in *Journal of Islamic Science* (Aligarh: The Muslim Association for the Advancement of Science, January 1985), vol. 1 no. 1.
20. Sayili, Aydin, "The Emergence of the Prototype of the Modern Hospital" in *Studies in History and Medicine* (Tughlaqabad, New Delhi: Department of History of Medicine and Medical Research, June 1980).
21. al Sharabassi, Ahmad, "Islam and Family Planning" in *Muslim Attitudes toward Family Planning*, ed. Olivia Schieffelin (New York: The Population Council, 1973).
22. Simpson, N.E., et al. "Prenatal Diagnosis of Genetic Disease" in *Canada: Report of a Collaborative Study* (Med. Assoc. J. 115:739, 1976).
23. Suzuki, David, "Life at All Cost is Too High a Price" in *Reader's Digest* (South Africa: Reader's Digest Association (Pty) Ltd., November 1985).
24. Vernet, J. "Ibn Hubal" in *The Encyclopaedia of Islam*, ed. B. Lewis, et al. (Leiden: E.J. Bill, 1971, New Edition).
25. Watson, R.A. "Urologic Complications of Legal Abortion" in *New Perspectives on Human Abortion*, ed. T.W. Hilgers, et al. (Lanham, Maryland: University Press of America Inc., 1981).
26. Wild, Jennifer, "Rape, abortion and our inadequate legal system" in *Sunday Tribune* (Durban, November 13, 1983).
27. "Test-tube Babies not the Answer" in *The Daily News* (Durban, November 22, 1982).
28. "Children's Right to Legitimacy" in *The Daily News* (Durban, eptember 12, 1984).
29. "Womb Leasing Causes Row" in *The Natal Mercury* (Durban, May 23, 1984).
30. "Report Claims Men React to Porn and Violence" in *The Daily News* (Durban, August 30, 1984).
31. "The Price of Promiscuity" in *Sunday Times Magazine* (Durban, May 12, 1985).

INDEX